From Vatican II to Pope Francis

From Vatican II to Pope Francis

Charting a Catholic Future

Edited by
PAUL CROWLEY, S.J.

ORBIS BOOKS

Maryknoll, New York 10545

ORBIS BOOKS
Maryknoll, New York 10545

Fathers and Brothers
MARYKNOLL™

Founded in 1970, Orbis Books endeavors to publish works that enlighten the mind, nourish the spirit, and challenge the conscience. The publishing arm of the Maryknoll Fathers and Brothers, Orbis seeks to explore the global dimensions of the Christian faith and mission, to invite dialogue with diverse cultures and religious traditions, and to serve the cause of reconciliation and peace. The books published reflect the views of their authors and do not represent the official position of the Maryknoll Society. To learn more about Maryknoll and Orbis Books, please visit our website at www. maryknollsociety.org.

Library of Congress Cataloging-in-Publication Data

From Vatican II to Pope Francis : charting a Catholic future / Paul Crowley, SJ, editor.
       pages cm
    Includes bibliographical references and index.
    ISBN 978-1-62698-089-1 (pbk.)
    1. Vatican Council (2nd : 1962-1965 : Basilica di San Pietro in Vaticano)
2. Catholic Church—Doctrines. I. Crowley, Paul G.
    BX8301962 .F76   2014
    282.09'046—dc23
                                                      2014010171

*Dedicated to the Dominicans
of the Catholic Community at Stanford*

Contents

Future Directions for the Church

Preface

Whenever I'm in a group of Catholic Christians who try to write a mission statement I have to fight the urge to dive out the nearest window. Didn't Jesus supply us with all the mission we'll ever need at the end of Matthew's Gospel? It's often called the Great Commission. It's addressed to the eleven disciples, which should be a big tipoff right away. Disciple is the Greek word for student, and that's an important word to me. I've been a Catholic campus minister working with college students for twenty-five years. Jesus gathers us in this very odd incomplete number. Who buys eleven eggs or eleven doughnuts or eleven of anything? In college football this is the twelfth-man tradition. We don't sit watching from the sidelines. Following Jesus is not a spectator sport. The Spirit of the Risen Christ urges us to say, "Put me in, Coach."

When we make ourselves available to the Spirit we're given authority—all of us are, by virtue of our baptism. We're given a completely universal mandate: go everywhere and make disciples of everyone. We're to do it in the power of the Father, the Son, and the Holy Spirit given us in baptism and to do everything with great love, which is the greatest and the root of all the commandments. Most importantly, we're reminded that Jesus is with us always and forever.

How do we do this on the non-Catholic college campuses where 90% of American Catholic college students study? We don't have easy access to the theologians who are found at Catholic universities.

A few years ago at the Catholic Community at Stanford we began to dream of something whose working title has been the Center for Theological and Spiritual Formation. Of course we did what people do when forming something new: we wrote a mission statement. We noted that in recent years an indoctrinational evangelical catechesis has emerged relying heavily on the 1994 Universal Catechism of the

Catholic Church as both the first and last word on any issue. Because time is always an issue for busy college students, especially those in preprofessional or advanced degree programs, short simple answers to complex questions can be superficially attractive. In such a context, the common student question, "Will this be on the test?" easily morphs into the plea, "Just tell me what I need to know." If we take this short cut, we give the world the last thing it needs, more religious fundamentalists.

As we planned for the 2012-13 academic year we noted that the fiftieth anniversary of the convening of the Second Vatican Council would occur in October 2012. "What if we created a two-day symposium?" we thought. We formed a team and brainstormed the topics we thought would need to be addressed. We decided to take our idea to Dr. Hester Gelber, then chair of Stanford's Department of Religious Studies. We brought our little outlines and nervously pitched our idea. We were hoping she might authorize some funding that would make our little project possible.

When she looked up from the outline we'd given her she said, "This isn't a symposium."

The voices in my head said, "Too bad. Well, at least we tried." Dr. Gelber spoke over them. "What you have here is a course. Would you consider partnering with our department and offering this as a ten-week course? We could supply the funding."

We did consider it, for about a nanosecond, and said yes to her offer. We had the two day symposium, which created greater interest in the course. We wanted to make sure that the students were drawn from the three generations that have lived with the effects of Vatican II. We were able to pick experts from all over the country. Almost all the lectures would be videotaped (and can now be accessed at catholic.stanford. edu.) And just as we began publicizing the course, hoping to fill a large lecture hall, there was suddenly big news from Rome. In a break with a 600-year tradition, the reigning pontiff resigned. Suddenly all eyes were on the window at the balcony in St. Peter's Square. The new pope appeared. Like St. Francis he preached without words. He didn't speak a blessing but asked for the world's silent blessing of him.

Our course drew as many as 110 students of all ages, averaging around 85 any given night. There were lectures and respondent panels, free exchange of ideas and extra optional sessions over lunch. It warmed my campus minister heart.

So, now it's your turn to be the disciple, the student. I hope you'll enjoy learning from those who offered their expertise to us.

Nathan G. Castle, O.P.
Director, Catholic Community at Stanford

Beyond Vatican II
Toward a Church of Yes

It makes me so happy. To be at the beginning again, and know-
ing almost nothing. . . . A door like this has cracked open five or six
times since we got up on our hind legs. It's the best possible time to
be alive, when almost everything you thought you knew is wrong.
—Tom Stoppard, *Arcadia*[1]

As I write these words, the Catholic Church is peering through a door cracked open by a new pope who has sparked the imagination of the world and rekindled a spirit of hope that many Catholics first encountered during the years of the Second Vatican Council (1962-65). For many, it seems that we are "at the beginning again," and, if not finding everything we thought we knew to be wrong, at least reassessing any number of assumptions about what we thought to be the norm for Catholicism as things had developed under the pontificates of John Paul II and Benedict XVI.

It is too early to make reliable judgments about what is going on, and it is too tempting to take any number of Francis's words and gestures to mean what we want them to mean, depending on what we want to see for the church in the "modern world." But one thing is by now patently clear: Francis, who was ordained after the close of the Council, wants to revive within the church the spirit with which Pope John XXIII opened the Council on that crisp October day in 1962. And here is one of the key passages that seems to be inspiring Francis's ministry:

> Nowadays . . . the spouse of Christ prefers to make use of the medicine of mercy rather than that of severity. She considers

---

1. Tom Stoppard, *Arcadia* (London: Faber & Faber, 1993), 47-48.

that she meets the needs of the present day by demonstrating the validity of her teaching rather than by condemnations. . . . That being so, the Catholic Church, raising the torch of religious truth by means of this ecumenical council, desires to show herself to be the loving mother of all, benign, patient, full of mercy and goodness toward the children separated from her. To the human race, oppressed by so many difficulties, she says like Peter of old to the poor man who begged alms from him: "Silver and gold I have none; but what I have, that I give thee. In the name of Jesus Christ of Nazareth, arise and walk" (Acts 3:6). . . . She opens the fountain of her life-giving doctrine which allows men, enlightened by the light of Christ, to understand well what they really are, what their lofty dignity and their purpose are, and, finally, through her children, she spreads everywhere the fullness of Christian charity, than which nothing is more effective in eradicating the seeds of discord, nothing more efficacious in promoting concord, just peace and the brotherly unity of all.[2]

This, it seems, offers many of the tonal notes of the Franciscan papacy to date: A call to mercy as the overarching context for the consideration of all things doctrinal and disciplinary; teaching through a demonstration of love and inclusion, rather than reiteration of formulas; a humility in pastoral service and a church marked by the poverty of the gospel; a focus on the frontiers of love, where many have been languishing; and, through all of these means, rather than by "the arm of severity," realizing the church as an instrument of peace, justice, and unity in the world. When we understand the "Johannine" foundation of this papacy, it is easier to understand how Francis could utter his now famous words, "Who am I to judge?"

But the foundations of this papacy are not only Johannine. They are also conciliar. In his path-breaking interview with Jesuit journals in September 2013, the pope was forceful about the contemporary impact of the Second Vatican Council:

---

2. "Mother Church Rejoices" (*Gaudet mater ecclesia*), address of Pope John XXIII at the opening of the Second Vatican Council, October 11, 1962, available at the Conciliaria website, conciliaria.com.

Vatican II was a re-reading of the Gospel in light of contemporary culture. . . . Vatican II produced a renewal movement that simply comes from the same Gospel. Its fruits are enormous. Just recall the liturgy. The work of liturgical reform has been a service to the people as a re-reading of the Gospel from a concrete historical situation. Yes, there are hermeneutics of continuity and discontinuity, but one thing is clear: the dynamic of reading the Gospel, actualizing its message for today—which was typical of Vatican II—is absolutely irreversible.[3]

He acknowledges here that there are differences of opinion over the correct theological interpretation of the Council, a debate that sharpened in the years leading up to his pontificate. Francis does not enter that particular debate, but rather expands the terms: the Council calls for a "dynamic reading of the Gospel" that will not allow us to remain settled in our ways, whether we see the Council as an exercise in continuity or discontinuity with the past. The guiding principle of the Council is to read the gospel "in light of contemporary culture." This does not mean simply adopting wholesale whatever contemporary culture might seem to dictate, but it does not automatically imply, either, that contemporary culture is the enemy, a culture of death. There are some cultural developments that might call for the church's careful and humble attention, for in those places, strange as they may seem, the Spirit might well be at work.

Such was the message in one of Francis's morning homilies at Domus Sanctae Marthae on May 2, 2013. The text was Acts 15:7-21, and the occasion was the Memorial of St. Athanasius, whose theology eventually led to ecclesial consensus at Nicea. Acts 15 concerns the meeting in Jerusalem at which parties in the primitive church were debating whether or not to require observance of the Mosaic law as a necessary part of witness to faith in Jesus Christ.[4] "There was a 'No' church that said, 'you cannot; no, no, you must not' and a 'Yes' church that said, 'but . . . let's think about it, let's be open to this, the Spirit

---

3. "A Big Heart Open to God," *America* (September 30, 2013): 15-38, at 30.
4. "Pope: A Church That Says Yes," available on the Vatican Radio website, en.radio.vaticana.va.

is opening the door to us.'" And what does it mean, this spirit of yes? It means that we must be willing to second-guess reflex responses to dig in our heels and ignore what is going on in contemporary culture in the name of a purity of faith. For the yes the pope speaks of is an assent to the Spirit who will save us from any "absolutizing instinct"[5] that would effectively narrow our vision:

> We ask the Lord that the Holy Spirit help us always to become a community of love, of love for Jesus who loved us so much. A community of this "yes." And from this "yes" the commandments are fulfilled. A community of open doors. And it defends us from the temptation to become perhaps Puritans, in the etymological sense of the word, to seek a para-evangelical purity, from being a community of "no." Because Jesus asks us first for love, love for Him, and to remain in His love.

Francis is adopting here the conciliar vision of an inclusive church, one that reaches out with "motherly" arms to embrace all, even when there are differences of interpretation. But, at the same time, there is a decided commitment to the freedom and detachment from ourselves and our preset opinions, whatever those may be, to which the gospel summons us. We must, the pope urges, become a community of love, of open doors, of yes to the Spirit. With words and dramatic gestures, Francis is signaling that we are at the beginning again, and that the door has indeed been cracked open.

*   *   *   *   *

When I was planning the symposium and course on Vatican II with the pastoral team of the Catholic Community at Stanford, Stanford's

---

5. On the "absolutizing instinct, " see William Lynch, *Images of Hope: Imagination as Healer of the Hopeless* (Notre Dame, IN: University of Notre Dame Press, 1965), 106: "Whatever is seen (or wished) as an absolute through the glasses of this instinct receives an enormous discharge of phantasy. The absolutizing instinct magnifies. In its presence each thing loses its true perspective and its true edges. The good becomes the tremendously good, the evil becomes the absolutely evil, the grey becomes the black or white, the complicated, because it is difficult to handle, becomes, in desperation, the completely simple. The small becomes the big."

Department of Religious Studies, and Stanford Continuing Studies, we had no idea, of course, that that door was to be cracked open again. Our aim was to commemorate the fiftieth anniversary of the Council on the Stanford campus, and to make of it an interdisciplinary academic event that would highlight the Council's history and achievements, while opening up further and deepening the question of how to interpret the Council in the present day. From the very beginning, we were insistent that the focus of the course not simply be on the past, on what the Council accomplished, but on what some of these accomplishments might portend for the future when viewed within the *present* context, which is decidedly different from the context of fifty years ago. With the help of a generous grant from the Rosemary Hewlett Fund of the Department of Religious Studies, we were able to hold a one-day symposium, followed by a quarter-long course open to Stanford students and occasional visitors from the Catholic Community at Stanford. We were greatly abetted by the wealth of resources available to us from the Religious Studies Departments at both Stanford and Santa Clara. The planning proceeded apace.

Then, on the eve of the symposium and the course, Francis was elected. It was too early then, even more so than now, to know what to make of some of his initial words and gestures, or to know in quite what direction we were starting to move. But this historical development did, in the long run, have an effect upon our thinking about the ultimate aim of the course by further considering what impact Francis might have for our reflection on the Council and its possible implications for the future. Suddenly there was a new factor to consider—the "Francis effect"—to the degree that we could make any sense of it at that early stage.

The present book, then, reflects partly what was offered in the Stanford course, but recrafted in light of directions indicated by the new papacy. The aim of this book is to get some kind of indication, in broad strokes, of how the promise of the Council might be realized in the future, as read from the present vantage point. Like the symposium and the course, the viewpoint is not so much retrospective and historical as it is proleptic and visionary. That viewpoint does not depend on what little we really do know of the new papacy at this moment; but its considerations are colored by the new atmosphere created by a pope who so resoundingly endorses reading the Council within the context of contemporary culture and who urges an openness to the Spirit that results in a church of "yes" to where that Spirit leads us.

In such an ambitious undertaking it was impossible in a short time to cover every imaginable topic in the kind of depth that scholars of the Council and others might desire. So, instead, we had to be selective, focusing on those documents and themes that continue to energize our imaginations. Some topics that were covered in the Stanford course, such as liturgical renewal, are not included in this volume. Others, such as imagining new forms of ministry, were not deeply addressed in the course. What we do have here is a unified collection of thought around where the inspirations of the Council might take us in the future, but with different tasks assigned to each thought exercise. Thus, the volume is divided into three parts: "Contemporary Contexts" for reading the Council today, "Recasting Conciliar Achievements" with a view toward how things have changed in fifty years, and "Future Directions for the Church" with an eye on the directions in which Francis seems to be leading us.

Even apart from the surprise of a new pope, it is important to pay due heed to the contemporary cultural and religious contexts within which we read the Council fifty years later, as these factors affect greatly the final shape of our thinking about the future. Three highly creative scholars help us to sketch in the broad lines of the contemporary context, at least as viewed from the perspective of those involved in this enterprise from an academic grounding in the United States. This was a necessary selection, but all three of these essays are rooted in the experience of the global Catholic Church in the past fifty years, during a time when the church in the United States has become increasingly aware of its particular but not necessarily normative role in the world church.

Stephen Schloesser sets the stage for a contemporary approach to the conciliar documents by shifting the typical emphasis away from the context of the Council itself, the 1960s aftermath of the Second World War, the fall of colonialism, and the emergence of the East–West axis, to a situation the Council fathers could never have imagined: the "biopolitics" of gender, sexuality, feminism, sexual identity, and shifting family gestalts, as well as the birth control, abortion, and bioethics debates that have come together to form a major locus of cultural energy in the decades since the Council. The Council fathers could scarcely have known that they were "dancing on the edge of a volcano" about to erupt into this array of issues. They were meeting at a turning point in history, at that very moment when the turning was so deep that it seemed not to be happening. But there were rumblings far below. And the decades following the Council were to see a virtually worldwide explosion, starting with the Pill, already in the air at the Council, but proscribed from discussion. It is little surprise that the family is the topic for the first synod to be called by Francis, as opposed, say, to a more theological topic such as faith in God in the face of contemporary atheism, which might have been expected in 1965. Schloesser places this newly formed horizon face to face with the horizon of the Council and establishes a hermeneutical framework for reading the Council today and carrying its program into the foreseeable future. This program concerns not so much an exegesis of the texts as mid-twentieth-century documents, although this part of any hermeneutic is essential, as an illumination of the texts in the new light of the "biopolitical" context within which we live today.

Schloesser's thesis is amplified in Sally Vance-Trembath's essay on the situation of women in the aftermath of Vatican II. As she convincingly argues, the problematic situation for women in the church runs deeper than the question of whether or not women are to be granted all seven sacraments. The situation of women in society and in the church, scarcely addressed in any direct fashion by the Council itself, is now an indispensable framework within which the Council's achievements must be interrogated, interpreted from the vantage point of the present day, and deployed for the future. Again, the Council fathers could not have imagined the massive shifts that were about to take place in wider society, and not only in the West, with regard to the roles of women and women's self-understanding. Nor could they have imagined the massive sociological shifts, especially in the West, that Catholicism was to undergo in the next fifty years, the topic treated by sociologist of religion Jerome Baggett. Although we do find references to the modern age in the Council documents, and a fairly exhaustive survey of the modern world in *Gaudium et spes*, there was as yet no cognizance of the shifts that were already beginning to take place within Catholicism and its relation to wider culture. Yet, if we are to

ask the Council to speak to the present age, and to the future, and if
the church is indeed to become a community of yes in any intelligent
way, then these shifts must be taken into account, not only as problems, but as raw data—the real life within which the Spirit is beckon-
ing the church forward. Thus, the fact that the people of God largely
have not received church teaching prohibiting artificial birth control or
the fact that there have been massive declines in identification with the
Catholic Church in Western societies might actually present opportunities for creative evangelization—as Pope Francis seems to have
gleaned—rather than a reflex rhetoric of denunciation or the erection
of ecclesiastical barriers to ensure doctrinal purity.

These preliminary contextual essays allow for a closer look at five
Council documents that continue to resonate today: *Lumen gentium*
(Dogmatic Constitution on the Church), *Dei verbum* (Dogmatic
Constitution on Divine Revelation), *Gaudium et spes* (Pastoral Constitution on the Church in the Modern World), *Dignitatis humanae*
(Declaration on Religious Freedom), and *Nostra aetate* (Declaration
on Non-Christian Religions). In each of these essays parts of these
documents are mined for their effects on the postconciliar era and for
future directions that they might indicate for a church open to the
continuing work of the Spirit.

Archbishop Emeritus John R. Quinn leads with a proposal seemingly dear to the heart and program of Pope Francis: the invigoration
of structures of collegiality and of ecclesial communion—in short,
a more decentralized church structure in keeping with the ancient
structures of communion of the first centuries. This was the promise of *Lumen gentium*, but it has remained largely unrealized. Yet current calls by the pope for a recovery of "synodality" as a key feature
of church governance rely on the kind of vision represented by the
archbishop's prodigious work in this area,[6] which seems to have been
added to the pope's reading list.

Yet no vitality can be hoped for if it is not infused by a living contact
with the Word of God, and here Barbara Green reminds us of the
historic proportions of the opening of the Scriptures made possible

---

6. See his recent work, *Ever Ancient, Ever New: Structures of Communion in
the Church* (Mahwah, NJ: Paulist Press, 2013).

by *Dei verbum*. The implications are even deeper than the qualified Roman acceptance of Reformation doctrine on the privileged role of Scripture in the life of the church. Due to the remarkably deep embrace of secular methods for the interpretation of the sacred text, we find here a model for the church's engagement with the world in the future, which requires a mind open to the discovery of the implications of truth as yet unknown. With some irony we note that it was the Pontifical Biblical Commission that concluded to a theological *aporia* on the question of the ordination of women—a stance of intellectual honesty that the church could do well to adopt as we move into the future with regard to this and other challenging topics.

Likewise, *Gaudium et spes* unleashed for the church a torrent of the Spirit, as the church in various parts of the world endeavored to actualize the call of the Pastoral Constitution for ecclesial solicitude toward the poor and oppressed of our societies. This was to develop, as we know, into the declaration of the church's "preferential option for the poor" and for the further development of Catholic social doctrine, starting with the courageous teaching of Pope Paul VI in *Populorum progressio* and *Octogesima adveniens*. Bryan Massingale traces the impact of this teaching on the church's participation in the civil rights movement and racial equality in general, while Kristin Heyer focuses on the implications of the Council's vision on current debates over health care and immigration, the latter a topic that has been joined in recent months by Pope Francis. The new era for the church begun by *Gaudium et spes* is hardly finished, as past breakthroughs of the Spirit serve as harbingers of possible cultural and political watersheds where the church, as pastors and laity working together, will again be called to serve as gospel witness. The message here is that there can be no going back, no retreat into a narcissistic church that does not get its hands (and vestments!) dirty in doing the work of the gospel.

And this calls for a form of religious liberty in the marketplace of the world that, while treasuring the faith handed down through the generations, is rooted in and thrives within a secular world of democratic values and religious pluralism. Here J. Leon Hooper, one of the leading experts on the thought of American Jesuit John Courtney Murray, the architect of *Dignitatis humanae*, demonstrates the unique contribution of the United States to the church's current self-understanding, however contested it might be in some circles still. This document calls for religious liberty not only in civil societies but, in a certain sense, within the church itself. What this document really enshrines, it seems to me, is the central insight of the doctrine of the Incarnation itself, which is that the divine and the human met in a unity that did not destroy the integrity of the other. And so, the church can best navigate future waters with an embrace, however critical it may be, of the structures of democratic pluralism that guarantee religious liberty.

It is this very liberty that serves as the tacit presupposition for that remarkable document *Nostra aetate*, which declares the church's openness to the unique integrity of other religions, recognizing in some of them a "ray of the truth" that enlightens all human beings. Even more than the Declaration on Ecumenism, this declaration would raise to the fore some of the most central doctrines of Christian faith, not least the salvific role of Jesus Christ for all humankind, a claim that can seem overly bold within the context of a religious pluralism that is the accepted context for the church's contemporary life. Catherine Cornille calls here for an intellectual humility before those questions that the Council itself seemed to leave open and unsettled. A certain epistemological modesty, or agnosticism, rightly accompanies a humble posture for the church in regard to other religious traditions.

These essays set the stage for the final four of the book, which examine from different points of view future trajectories for Catholicism. The first, by Paul Lakeland, addresses the roles of the laity in the future church and establishes those roles in baptism, by which all, not only the ordained, are joined to the priesthood of Christ. This kind of thinking will require a number of attitudinal and possibly doctrinal shifts in our understanding of the ordained priesthood, as Francis himself has indicated in his severe criticisms of clericalism and power-based theologies of ordination. Here William Ditewig takes up the cause, urging a consideration of new approaches to the theology of ordination itself—one that would result in more inclusivity in ministry and the disappearance of exclusivist claims of sacerdotal privilege. Both of these essays point us toward a future in which our understanding of ministry in the Catholic Church must be more radically transformed. It would seem that only in tandem with such a radical reinterpretation of ordination can difficult and vexing questions, such as the ordination of women to the diaconate, be adequately comprehended as a theological matter.

The future for the church also depends on the effective participation and ownership by each Catholic of the tradition that has been handed on. And this means that "conscience" must be treasured. The seeds for a doctrine of conscience were indeed planted at the Council, but there has been in subsequent years a certain loss of nerve on the part of some of the church's teachers in further developing this ancient tradition. David DeCosse asks how a retrieval of the sanctity of conscience (and the receptivity to the Spirit that that would require) could help the church face the future with the kind of openness that Francis seeks to inspire. Yet, as he notes, conscience is not merely an individual possession; within the church it is an ecclesial reality as well. The whole of the people of God move forward together into the future, aiding and assisting one another in the formation of a conscience that corresponds to discerning minds and hearts.

And so, to conclude the book, Albert and Barbara Gelpi call for a retrieval of the ancient doctrine of the *sensus fidelium*, that life of faith which at once enables Catholics to "be of one deep mind with the church" (*sentire cum ecclesiae*), as Ignatius of Loyola put it, and, as part of that thinking, to respond to the promptings of the Spirit that would move us forward, without fear, to become a community of love, a church of yes. They sum up beautifully here the future trajectories of the Council that could be realized if we summon the courage to accept the call to move forward.

It is my hope that this book will help Catholics to imagine the future of our church in a period in which the inspirations of the Second Vatican Council are being called upon again to populate our imaginations with images of hope. But those images for our time and our future will be different from the images that were imagined in the mid-twentieth century. It is our privileged task and opportunity together to chart a course for the Catholic future.

* * * * *

This book is the fruit of many labors. Several people at the Catholic Community at Stanford deserve special mention: Fr. Nathan Castle, O.P., Pastor and Director of the Catholic Community at Stanford, for suggesting the course; Nancy Greenfield, Chaplain for the Catholic Community at Stanford, without whose unfailing and prodigious work the symposium and course simply would not have happened; Sister Ramona Bascom, O.P., of the Catholic Community at Stanford staff, who was part of the planning from the beginning and who offered very helpful suggestions along the way; M'Lis Berry, whose computer expertise greatly abetted the delivery of course content to the Web; John Kerrigan, deacon to the Catholic Community at Stanford, whose support and help were stalwart as always; and Gary Glover, who provided technical assistance.

On the academic side of the street, I am especially indebted to Professor Hester Gelber, who was then Chair of the Religious Studies Department at Stanford. Professor Gelber arranged for the funding of the course through the Rosemary Hewlett Fund, and was generous with her time and suggestions for course improvements. Professor Steven Weitzman, the Daniel E. Koshland Professor of Jewish Culture and Religion at Stanford, participated in the panel on interreligious dialogue, and Professor Thomas Sheehan of the Religious Studies Department provided office accommodation for the quarter. Religious Studies Department staff, in particular Sunny Toy, Vera Haugh and Alberto Martin, made things work behind the scenes. I am equally indebted to Dan Colman, Associate Dean and Director of Stanford Continuing Studies, and to Liz Frith, Program and Planning Manager for Stanford Continuing Studies, who imaginatively made the course work with their students as well as with Stanford undergraduates. At Santa Clara, my thanks go to Gary Macy, the John Nobili Professor of Theology and Department Chair, who arranged my schedule so that I could shuttle between the nearby Stanford and Santa Clara campuses.

The following people, in addition to those included in this book, are to be thanked for their participation in the symposium or the course: Bishop Emeritus John Cummins of Oakland; Rosemary Ellmer, Ph.D., Counseling and Psychological Services, Santa Clara University; Mark Francis, C.V., President of the Catholic Theological Union, Chicago, and, at the time, Visiting Scholar at the Ignatian Center for Jesuit Education at Santa Clara; Anne Grycz, former Director of the Institute for Leadership in Ministry, Diocese of San José; Sister

Gloria Jones, O.P., Congregational Prioress of the Dominican Sisters of Mission San José; Akiba Lerner, Assistant Professor in Religious Studies, Santa Clara University; David M. Kennedy, the Donald J. McLachlan Professor of History, Emeritus, Stanford; Mahboob Khan, Director of Outreach and Events of Naqshbandi Sufi Order of the San Francisco Bay Area; Sally Mahoney, former Stanford Registrar; Scotty McLennan, Dean for Religious Life at Stanford; Professor Catherine Murphy, Religious Studies, Santa Clara University; and Catherine Wolff, Catholic Community at Stanford.

Finally, I would like to thank my research assistant, Angela Hollar, a graduate student at the Jesuit School of Theology of Santa Clara University. Without her professionalism, competence, organization, and faithful reliability, this project would not have lifted off the ground.

This book is dedicated to my Dominican friends and their pastoral coworkers at Stanford who have done so much to bring together the resources of the Catholic community of the Bay Area to establish an ecumenical, interfaith, and academic Catholic presence at Stanford. And they have done much to rekindle long-standing cooperative associations between Stanford and Santa Clara. May God prosper their work.

* * * * *

Editorial note: Except where noted, Council documents and papal speeches or documents are taken from the Vatican website (www. vatican.va). Where necessary, translations have been corrected for gender-inclusive usage.

Contemporary Contexts

1

"Dancing on the Edge of the Volcano"
Biopolitics and What Happened
after Vatican II

STEPHEN R. SCHLOESSER, S.J.

It is not the consciousness of men that determines their existence, but their social existence that determines their consciousness. . . . What else does the history of ideas prove, than that intellectual production changes its character in proportion as material production is changed? —Karl Marx[1]

A prophetic warning about matters that then had no name . . . a civilization that was unwittingly dancing on the edge of the volcano due to destroy it a few years hence. —Harry Halbreich[2]

Portentous events in 1963 would shape the future of American Catholicism: the death of Pope John XXIII, the election of Pope Paul VI, the March on Washington, and the assassination of President John F. Kennedy. Against the horizon of these world-historical

---

1. Karl Marx, Preface to *A Contribution to the Critique of Political Economy* (1859); and Marx and Friedrich Engels, *The Communist Manifesto* (1848); in *Karl Marx: Selected Writings*, ed. Lawrence Hugh Simon (Indianapolis: Hackett, 1994), 209-13, at 211; 157-86, at 174.

2. Harry Halbreich, *Arthur Honegger*, trans. Roger Nichols (Portland, OR: Amadeus Press, 1999), 417; quoted in Deborah Mawer, "'Dancing on the Edge of the Volcano': French Music in the 1930s," in *French Music since Berlioz*, ed. Richard Langham Smith and Caroline Potter (Aldershot, UK/Burlington, VT: Ashgate, 2006), 249-80, at 249.

events, two other events—both publications—seem small by comparison. And yet, they too were about to change the destiny of American Catholicism. The first was the promulgation of *Sacrosanctum concilium*, the first document of the Second Vatican Council, on December 4, just about two weeks after the Kennedy assassination. In retrospect, it can be seen as a long-duration coming to terms with the Renaissance and Reformation turn to vernacular languages. In the short-term duration, it can be seen as an effect of the violent global decolonization taking place since 1945. The second was Betty Friedan's *The Feminine Mystique*, which was published earlier that year on February 19. A touchstone moment in "second-wave feminism," Friedan's work heralded an unprecedented epoch in the history of gender relations, one in which we live today.

These two publication events signal a curious fact about the Second Vatican Council: on the one hand, it accommodated itself to several centuries of change preceding it (the Reformation, the French Revolution, nineteenth-century nationalism and liberalism). On the other hand, it seems to have been woefully inadequate to the most important epistemic shift of the twentieth century: biopolitics and biopower.[3] Vatican Council II can be viewed as suspended between two

---

3. I first became attracted to this concept in 2010 while rewriting an earlier presentation for publication: "I would prefer to use the terms 'biopower' and 'biopolitics.' They appeal to me more than 'sexuality,' 'gender,' 'reproduction,' and 'bioethics' because they unify issues surrounding human interactions with 'life'—'bios'—on the planetary as well as individual levels. Today's most urgent emerging 'life' questions are 'environmental' questions, i.e., about the very possibility of future life on earth. But even here, as radio host Krista Tippett has recently observed, our emerging awareness transcends more limited categories like 'sexuality' and 'ecology': 'It's been striking how, across the past few years, the environment has found its way inside my guests' reflections on every subject, as they say, under the sun. And we do need fresh vocabulary and expansive modes of reflection on this subject that, we've come to realize, is not just about ecology but the whole picture of human life and lifestyle.' Perhaps Pope Benedict XVI will indeed be remembered as a 'green' Pope." See Stephen Schloesser, "Jesuit Hybrids, Catholic Moderns, Futural Pasts," in *For the City and the World: Conversations in Catholic Studies and Social Thought (Lane Center Lectures 2005-2010)*, ed. Julia Dowd (San Francisco: University of San Francisco Press/Association of Jesuit University Presses, 2010), 114-41, at 139n77.

epochs. Behind it: the Second World War, the Holocaust, the Cold War, and decolonization. Before it: contraception, abortion, gay rights, and stem cell research. Behind it: long-standing issues of traditional politics. Before it: largely unexplored territory of biopolitics. Looking back: confident culmination. Lying ahead: moral panic.[4]

The years 1962-1965 were not like indistinguishable four-year periods. As a divide severing past from future, the epoch instead resembles brief periods like the French Revolution and its Terror (1789-1793), the American Civil War (1861-1865), the Great War (1914-1918), and the Second World War (1939-1945). Being a time of relative geopolitical peace (a "cold" war), the chasm of 1962-1965 can appear deceptively unremarkable. However, viewed from fifty years on, the postconciliar cliff looms large on the horizon, especially after the pivotal American year of 1964.[5] To use another metaphor: as the Council celebrated its conclusion in December 1965, it was dancing on the edge of a volcano.

It is useful to distinguish between political and biopolitical issues. On the one hand, Vatican II summed up and responded to a world whose political conflicts had reached widely held conclusions.[6] Eight years prior to the Council's conclusion, the Battle of Algiers (1956-1957) signaled a high-water mark in violent postwar decolonization. In 1958, the title of Chinua Achebe's now iconic work, *Things Fall Apart*—published the same year as the collapse of France's postwar

---

4. Charles Krinsky, *The Ashgate Research Companion to Moral Panics* (Burlington, VT: Ashgate, 2013); Stanley Cohen, *Folk Devils and Moral Panics: The Creation of the Mods and Rockers*, 3rd ed. (New York: Routledge, [1972] 2002); Marshall McLuhan, *Understanding Media: The Extensions of Man* (New York: McGraw-Hill, 1964).

5. For a riveting account of the cultural turning point in 1964, see the following documentary film: Jon Margolis and Public Broadcasting Service (U.S.), *1964*, American Experience series (Arlington, VA: PBS, 2014); based on Jon Margolis, *The Last Innocent Year: America in 1964: The Beginning of the "Sixties"* (New York: William Morrow, 1999).

6. For a fuller exposition of the preconciliar context, see Stephen Schloesser, "Against Forgetting: Memory, History, Vatican II," in *Vatican II: Did Anything Happen?*, ed. John W. O'Malley, David G. Schultenover, Stephen Schloesser (New York: Continuum, 2007), 92-152.

Fourth Republic (over the Algerian crisis), the death of Pope Pius XII, and the newly inaugurated Soviet premier Nikita Khrushchev's commencement of de-Stalinization—nicely summed up the century's first half. In 1959, following the death of Pope Pius XII, German bishops finally began to issue their first statements on the Holocaust—nearly fifteen years after its conclusion.[7] In January 1961, the United Nations resolved to make the 1960s the "Decade of Development"; President Kennedy launched that decade nine months later in a visit to New York.[8] In 1962, Algeria gained independence. Decolonization was giving way to the postcolonial era.

On October 11, 1962, the Council opened on the very eve of the Cuban Missile Crisis (October 14-28), which threatened the planet with nuclear annihilation. In 1963, Rolf Hochhuth's play *The Deputy, a Christian Tragedy* (American translation, published 1964), opened the question of the late pontiff's role in the Holocaust and inaugurated the "Pius Wars" which have continued into the present. The Council responded to these political upheavals—the Holocaust, the Cold War, nuclear proliferation, and decolonization—in its considerations of non-Christian religions (particularly Judaism), religious liberty, democracy, freedom of conscience, atheism, and vernacular liturgical adaptations.[9] Seen from the standpoint of the preconciliar years, Vatican II successfully resolved a number of political issues that were both acutely twentieth century as well as long-durational, that is, effects of the Enlightenment, French Revolution, and nineteenth-century nationalist liberalism.

However, biopolitics was a different story. Vatican II seems to have been incognizant of, unprepared for, and inadequate to another set of issues that lay directly ahead—not so much traditional political issues (nationalism, racialism, imperialism) as biopolitical ones: companionate marriage and its necessary corollary of divorce and remarriage; the nuclear family as an emotional and not an economic unit (a shift from

---

7. Michael Phayer, *The Catholic Church and the Holocaust, 1930-1965* (Bloomington, IN: Indiana University Press, 2000), 200.

8. Address by President John F. Kennedy to the UN General Assembly, September 25, 1961; text available at the State Department website, www.state.gov. My thanks to Kenneth Himes.

9. See Schloesser, "Against Forgetting."

rural to urban economies); the extension of Enlightenment notions of equality to women; the complexity of sexual identities and relationships; and biomedical technologies capable of regulating reproduction, extending the life span, and enhancing the quality of life.[10]

A milestone in this biopolitical epoch occurred just seven months before Kennedy—a physically attractive icon of vigor and vitality (ironically so, given what is now known about his extreme chronic pain) and representing the generational succession of youth—would be elected president two years before the Council's opening. On May 9, 1960, the world's first commercially produced birth-control pill, Enovid-10, was approved by the U.S. Food and Drug Administration (FDA). This technological material production was soon followed by an intellectual production: Betty Friedan's *The Feminine Mystique* (1963), following the path opened by Simone de Beauvoir's landmark *The Second Sex* (1949). The two works are seen today as foundational moments of second-wave feminism.[11]

Just two and a half years after the Council closed in December 1965, Pope Paul VI promulgated his encyclical *Humanae vitae* (Of Human Life) in late July 1968. Looking back, a more ill-advised and ill-timed appearance is difficult to imagine. Lyndon B. Johnson's 1965 escalation of America's involvement in Vietnam had catalyzed the synergy of racial and generational turmoil that would become known as "The Sixties." The encyclical's launch coincided with a genuinely global collapse of trust in authority during the "Year that Rocked the World."[12] The Prague Spring began with the election of Alexander Dubček (January 5); Walter Cronkite delivered his shocking judgment on television that

---

10. Note, however, that thinkers like Michel Foucault and Giorgio Agamben would not make this distinction. Rather, they view biopower as the further extension of the modern bureaucratic state's surveillance and control into the innermost reaches of private life. Agamben, for example, "defines the concentration camp as the 'biopolitical paradigm of the West.'" See Thomas Lemke, *Biopolitics: An Advanced Introduction*, trans. Eric Frederick Trump (New York: New York University Press, 2011), 53; quoting Agamben, *Homo Sacer: Sovereign Power and Bare Life*, trans. Daniel Heller-Roazen (Stanford, CA: Stanford University Press, 1998), 181.

11. Stephanie Coontz, *A Strange Stirring: The Feminine Mystique and American Women at the Dawn of the 1960s* (New York: Basic Books, 2011).

12. Mark Kurlansky, *1968: The Year That Rocked the World* (New York: Ballantine, 2004).

the war in Vietnam was unwinnable (February 27); President Johnson, politically crippled by the war, announced late in the game that he would not seek reelection (March 31); several days later, Martin Luther King, Jr., was assassinated (April 4), and American cities exploded in race riots; partly in reaction to the short-term trigger of the Tet Offensive (January-February 1968), riots erupted in London, Paris, Berlin, and Rome between March and May; shortly afterward, Senator Robert F. Kennedy was assassinated (June 6). It is within this global cultural crisis that *Humanae vitae* was promulgated several weeks later on the feast of St. James the Apostle (July 25). It was followed one month later by the brutal Warsaw Pact suppression of the Prague Spring in Czechoslovakia (August 21) and by the riots marring Chicago's Democratic National Convention (August 26-29). Largely in reaction to a widespread perception of national societal collapse, Richard Nixon was elected on a law-and-order platform (November 5). A month later, Chairman Mao Zedong began his "Down to the Countryside Movement," the forced relocation of "young intellectuals" from urban areas to remote rural ones. In short: the summer of 1968 was an inauspicious moment in which to reassert authority with an unpopular encyclical.

The story of *Humanae vitae*, both its genesis and its fractious consequences for the church, has been told often and well.[13] The episode irreparably damaged Paul VI's own felt sense of authority. Although he had feverishly produced seven encyclicals in the first four years of his pontificate (1964-1967), he would not publish any during the next ten years between his eighth (*Humanae vitae*, July 1968) and his death (August 1978).[14]

---

13. Martine Sevegrand, *L'affaire* Humanae Vitae: *l'Église catholique et la contraception* (Paris: Karthala, 2008); Leslie Woodcock Tentler, *Catholics and Contraception: An American History* (Ithaca, NY: Cornell University Press, 2004); Robert McClory, *Turning Point: The Inside Story of the Papal Birth Control Commission, and How* Humanae vitae *Changed the Life of Patty Crowley and the Future of the Church* (New York: Crossroad, 1995); Fernando Vittorino Joannes, *The Bitter Pill: Worldwide Reaction to the Encyclical* Humanae Vitae, trans. IDOC [International Documentation and Communication Centre] (Philadelphia: Pilgrim Press, 1970); cf. John T. McGreevy's chapter "Life (I)," in *Catholicism and American Freedom: A History* (New York: W. W. Norton, 2003), 216-49.

14. Paul VI marked the eightieth anniversary of *Rerum novarum* with

After the summer of 1968, "The Sixties" marched on. The "Stone-wall riots" (June 28, 1969) would come to symbolize the inaugural moment of the gay liberation movement. (England and Wales had passed limited decriminalization of same-sexual activity in The Sexual Offences Act of 1967.) Although this particular civil rights movement was something of a latecomer after others in the "New Left" (African-American, feminist, Chicano, and antiwar), it would have unpredictably rapid consequences during the next three decades (due in no small part to the coming AIDS pandemic of the 1980s).[15] Four years later, the United States followed the lead of the United Kingdom's Abortion Act of 1967: the Supreme Court decision of *Roe v. Wade* legalized abortion on January 22, 1973. Two years later, France followed suit with the [Simone] Veil Law (1975). The linkage between the regulation of birth by nuclear families and worldwide concern over population growth had been explicitly expressed in *Gaudium et spes* in 1965.[16] Ten years later, governments in the developing world assumed control: India's family planning initiative began in April 1976; China introduced its one-child policy in 1978.[17]

Octogesima adveniens (May 14, 1971), not an encyclical but rather an apostolic letter.

15. For a succinct overview, see Van Gosse, *The Movements of the New Left, 1950-1975: A Brief History with Documents* (Boston: Bedford/St. Martin's, 2005).

16. Compare *Gaudium et spes:* "But there are many today who maintain that the increase in world population, or at least the population increase in some countries, must be radically curbed by every means possible and by any kind of intervention on the part of public authority. In view of this contention, the Council urges everyone to guard against solutions, whether publicly or privately supported, or at times even imposed, which are contrary to the moral law. . . . Men should discreetly be informed, furthermore, of scientific advances in exploring methods whereby spouses can be helped in regulating the number of their children and whose safeness has been well proven and whose harmony with the moral order has been ascertained" (*Gaudium et spes*, 87). Translations of all conciliar documents and papal encyclicals, exhortations, and addresses here and following have been taken from the Vatican website: http://www.vatican.va/.

17. For a darkly compelling reading, see Matthew James Connelly, *Fatal Misconception: The Struggle to Control World Population* (Cambridge, MA: Belknap Press of Harvard University Press, 2008).

Although an oversimplification, the story of Vatican II's afterlife might nevertheless be usefully imagined as a "tale of two encyclicals." On March 26, 1967, Paul VI had laid out his own progressive "Decade of Development" vision in *Populorum progressio* (On the Progress of Peoples). However, its effect was quickly blunted by the promulgation of its successor—*Humanae vitae*—just sixteen months later.[18] As a result, very soon after Vatican II's closure, the public face of Roman Catholicism came to be identified with the pro-life movement and anti-abortion political affiliations.[19] This innovation would gain even more momentum during the papacies following the death of Paul VI in August 1978: John Paul II (1978-2005) and Benedict XVI (2005-2013). Even as both pontiffs played strong roles in identifying Catholicism with anti-abortion forces, they simultaneously used institutional means to suppress varieties of post-1945 political (or "liberation") theologies that looked to Paul VI's writings (regardless of his intentions) for magisterial support. (See, for example, the "option for the poor" defined by the Second General Conference of the Latin American Bishops in Medellín, Colombia [1968].) In retrospect, 1979 appears as an unanticipated year of counterrevolution.[20]

In the rich accounts we now have of "What Happened at Vatican II," the Council appears to be in sync with the political spirit of its times and even occasionally prophetic in its inspirational epideictic rhetorical

---

18. For a similar juxtaposition of two encyclicals, one biopolitical and the other socio-economic, see *Casti connubii* (December 31, 1930) and *Quadragesimo anno* (May 15, 1931); discussed in Schloesser, "Jesuit Hybrids," 128-30.

19. See McGreevy chapter, "Life (II)," in *Catholicism and American Freedom*, 250-81. As Margaret A. Farley wrote in 2000: "Preoccupation with abortion has overshadowed all other issues important to the Church's political agenda. The consequences of this are visible not only in the strategies of the Church's leadership but in the responses of a vast majority of Church members." See Farley, "The Church in the Public Forum: Scandal or Prophetic Witness?," in Catholic Theological Society of America, *CTSA Proceedings* 55 (2000): 87-101, at 90. My thanks to Kenneth Himes.

20. Christian Caryl, *Strange Rebels: 1979 and the Birth of the 21st Century* (New York: Basic Books, 2013); Philip Jenkins, *Decade of Nightmares: The End of the Sixties and the Making of Eighties America* (New York: Oxford University Press, 2006).

style.[21] However, when we consider the biopolitical spirit of its times, the Council appears to be out of sync with, unconcerned with, and even unconscious of the currents that would soon become today's commonplaces. In terms of "history" and "memory," the political issues at the Council seem to be "historical." The legitimacy of democracy as a form of government, religious liberty, and Jewish dignity—all contested issues of the nineteenth- to mid-twentieth century—had been largely resolved by the mid-1960s. By contrast, biopolitical issues were and remain today marked by "memory" of the recent past and even the present.

As I write (in January 2014), German Chancellor Angela Merkel—arguably today's most powerful European head of state—has just handily won reelection. Park Geun-hye is the current president of South Korea; Cristina Kirchner the president of Argentina, and Dilma Vana Rousseff the president of Brazil. Previous heads of state have included Indira Gandhi (India, 1966-1977; 1980-1984), Golda Meir (Israel, 1969-1974), Margaret Thatcher (United Kingdom, 1975-1979), and Mary Robinson (Ireland, 1990-1997). For the past two years, the Managing Director of the International Monetary Fund (IMF) has been Christine Lagarde; and in the United States, Janet Yellen has just been named the first female chair of the Federal Reserve. Other recent occupants of national leadership roles have included Margaret Chase Smith, Barbara Jordan, Geraldine Ferraro, Madeleine Albright, Condoleezza Rice, Hillary Rodham Clinton, Diane Feinstein, Olympia Snowe, and Nancy Pelosi. During his brief time in office in 1978 (before his assassination), San Francisco Supervisor Harvey Milk was the first openly gay person to be elected to public office in California. In 1987, Barney Frank of Massachusetts became the first voluntarily and publicly self-identified gay man in Congress. In 2004, the Commonwealth of Massachusetts followed the lead of the Netherlands (2001) and Belgium (2003) in legalizing same-sex marriage. Spain quickly followed in 2005. As of this writing, fifteen nations recognize same-sex marriage (with the United Kingdom soon to follow), and another fifteen recognize other types of partnership. In the United

---

21. John W. O'Malley, *What Happened at Vatican II* (Cambridge, MA: Belknap Press of Harvard University Press, 2008); O'Malley, Schultenover, and Schloesser, eds., *Vatican II: Did Anything Happen?*

States, seventeen states and the District of Columbia recognize same-sex marriage. [*Editor's note:* As this book goes to press (June 2014), there are now twenty states that recognize same-sex marriage.]

In short: postconciliar Catholicism stands in stark contrast to bio-political realities since 1965—a vivid contrast tragically highlighted by the sexual abuse scandals since 2002. From a traditional political perspective, the Council's closure in December 1965—with the dec-larations on religious liberty (*Dignitatis humanae*) and non-Christian religions (*Nostra aetate*) as well as the promulgation of *Gaudium et spes*—reads as a triumph and even a comedy in the literary sense, that is, a final banquet of unity celebrating a reversal of fortunes. By contrast, from the biopolitical perspective, the same Council seems to have been unconscious of violent forces heating up beneath the sur-face:"dancing on the edge of the volcano" and largely silent about "mat-ters that then had no name."[22]

One way of accounting for this apparent blindness, inarticulate-ness, or deaf ear (depending on one's preferred metaphor) is to exag-gerate the unexpected suddenness and rupture of the "sexual revolu-tion" of "The Sixties." There is some truth in this view. The invention of the oral contraceptive was in fact unprecedented, a material produc-tion and conceptual precondition that had never before needed to be considered. The same might be said for various transatlantic decrimi-nalization acts: contraceptive devices (*Griswold v. Connecticut*, 1965), interracial marriage (*Loving v. Virginia*, 1967), abortion (United King-dom, 1967; *Roe v. Wade*, 1973; France, 1975), and sodomy (England and Wales, 1967; *Lawrence v. Texas*, 2003). Even the meaning of "bio-politics" as unveiling "life processes as a new object of political reflec-tion" did not emerge until the 1960s and early 1970s.[23]

---

22. Halbreich, *Arthur Honegger*, 417.

23. Lemke, *Biopolitics*, 23. For origins, see Michel Foucault, "Right of Death and Power over Life," in Paul Rabinow, ed., *The Foucault Reader* (New York: Pantheon Books, 1988), 258-72; Michel Foucault, "The Birth of Biopolitics," in *Ethics, Subjectivity and Truth: Essential Works of Foucault*, vol. 1, ed. P. Rabinow and J. D. Faubion (New York: New Press, 1997), 73-79; Michel Foucault, Lec-ture 11 (March 17, 1976), in *Society Must Be Defended: Lectures at the Collège de France, 1975-76*, ed. M. Bertani, A. Fontana, F. Ewald, and D. Macey (New York: Picador, 2003), 239-64. For an instructive overview, see Paul Rabinow and

However, although the intellectual production of such interpretative categories lagged behind material shifts, a massive and growing historiography on these biopolitical realities demonstrates long-duration trajectories that extend back through the 1950s (in Dagmar Herzog's felicitous phrase, "Sex after Fascism"), the Great Depression of the 1930s, and new possibilities (as well as repressions) in the postwar "Roaring Twenties."[24] Preconciliar theological reflection on the replacement of traditional marriage by companionate marriage serves as a case study.

Nikolas Rose, "Biopower Today," *BioSocieties* 1.2 (2006): 195-217. For a vision of the future, see Nikolas Rose, *The Politics of Life Itself: Biomedicine, Power, and Subjectivity in the Twenty-First Century* (Princeton, NJ: Princeton University Press, 2007). For the thought of Italian political theorist Roberto Esposito, see the special issue edited by Timothy Campbell entitled "Bios, Immunity, Life: The Thought of Roberto Esposito," *Diacritics* 36.2 (Summer 2006); and Esposito, *Bíos: Biopolitics and Philosophy*, trans. and with an introduction by Timothy Campbell (Minneapolis: University of Minnesota Press, 2008). I am grateful to Andrea Vicini, S.J., for directing me to Esposito's work.

24. Some of the earliest publications dating from 1980 to 1989 fell under the rubric "private life": Michael Anderson and Economic History Society, *Approaches to the History of the Western Family, 1500-1914* (London: Macmillan, 1980); Philippe Ariès and Georges Duby, eds., *A History of Private Life*, 5 vols. (Cambridge, MA: Belknap Press of Harvard University Press, 1987-1991), orig., *Histoire de la vie privée*, 5 vols. (Paris: Seuil, 1985-1987); John D'Emilio and Estelle B. Freedman, *Intimate Matters: A History of Sexuality in America* (New York: Harper & Row, 1988); Stephanie Coontz, *The Social Origins of Private Life: A History of American Families, 1600-1900* (New York: Verso, 1988); Roderick Phillips, *Putting Asunder: A History of Divorce in Western Society* (New York: Cambridge University Press, 1988); Mary Lyndon Shanley, *Feminism, Marriage, and the Law in Victorian England, 1850-1895* (Princeton, NJ: Princeton University Press, 1989); A. R. H. Copley, *Sexual Moralities in France, 1780-1980: New Ideas on the Family, Divorce, and Homosexuality: An Essay on Moral Change* (New York Routledge, 1989). Since 1990, marked especially by Thomas Laqueur's poststructuralist *Making Sex: Body and Gender from the Greeks to Freud* (Cambridge, MA: Harvard University Press, 1990), a proliferation of monographs have been published on numerous "biopolitical" topics: abortion, contraception, divorce, eugenics, family, feminism, fertility, gender, homosexuality, hygiene, marriage, masturbation, miscegenation, population, prostitution, queer politics, same-sex marriage, suffrage, transgender reassignment.

The groundwork for a new Catholic conception of marriage was produced throughout the 1930s, an unintended consequence of the growing transatlantic acceptance of contraception. As late as the Code of Canon Law promulgated in 1917 (just as the Great War was ending), drawing on the tradition of both Augustine and Aquinas, Canon 1013 had defined two "ends" (or purposes) of marriage: a primary end of "procreation and nurture of children" and a secondary end of "mutual help and the remedying of concupiscence."[25]

However, the 1914-18 cultural catastrophe had changed society and culture far more than anyone could have anticipated. The traditional Western European understanding of marriage—a preindustrial agrarian arrangement that viewed both children and the family as economic rather than emotional units—had been gradually fading away throughout the urbanizing and industrializing nineteenth century. (Cultural witnesses to its decline include Gustave Flaubert's *Madame Bovary* [1856]; Henrik Ibsen's *A Doll's House* [1879]; Leo XIII's *Arcanum* [On Christian Marriage, 1880]; Strindberg's *Miss Julie* [written 1888]; Ibsen's *Hedda Gabler* [1890].) The Great War definitively sealed this old world. After decades of struggle—for example, the French League for Women's Rights (1882) and the French Union for Women's Rights (1905)—women achieved suffrage toward the Great War's end and in the postwar era: for example, Canada (1917; Catholic Quebec in 1940), Germany's Weimar Republic (1918), Austria (1919), the United States (1920), and the United Kingdom (1918 partial; 1928 full). (France did not extend suffrage until the end of the German Occupation in 1944.)

By 1924, Abbé Jean Viollet had begun his ministry of answering couples' inquiries about sexuality (and especially contraception), and he published frequently on the topics of marriage, family, contraception, sterilization, and eugenics: *Education about Purity and Feeling* (1925), *Education by the Family* (1926), *Familial Morality* (1927), *The Duties of Marriage* (several editions by 1928), *Eugenics, Sterilization, Their Moral Value* (1929).[26] In Germany, the lay theologian Dietrich von Hildebrand

---

25. *Codex Iuris Canonici* (1917), 1013; quoted in Robert E. Obach, *The Catholic Church on Marital Intercourse: From St. Paul to Pope John Paul II* (Lanham, MD: Lexington Books, 2009), 121.

26. See works by Abbé Jean Viollet: *Éducation de la pureté et du sentiment*

published his books *Purity and Virginity* (1928) and *Marriage* (1929).[27] In July 1930, the Lambeth Conference opened; it would famously produce Resolution 15, a relaxation of Anglican attitudes toward birth control.[28] Pope Pius XI swiftly responded just five months later with the publication of *Casti connubii* (December 31, 1930). However, even as the encyclical prohibited both contraception and abortion, it invited new considerations of marriage as an emotional institution.

As a result, the 1930s would be filled with Catholic writings that attempted to reconcile tradition with modernity.[29] In France, Abbé Viollet published *Marriage* (1932), *The Psychology of Marriage* (1935), *Christian Law and Marriage* (1936).[30] Also in 1936, Hildebrand's *Marriage* (German, 1929) appeared in French translation with the

---

(Paris: Association du mariage chrétien, 1925); *L'éducation par la famille* (Paris: Association du mariage chrétien, 1926); *Morale familiale* (Paris: Association du mariage chrétien, 1927); *Les devoirs du mariage*, 4th ed. (Paris: Association du mariage chrétien, 1928). See also Jean Viollet et al., *Pour restaurer la famille* (Paris: Éditions de la S.A.P.E., 1927); Jean Viollet and André Lorulot, *L'Église et l'amour: controverse publique entre MM. l'abbé Viollet et André Lorulot* (Herblay [Seine et Oise]: Aux Éditions de "l'idée libre," 1929); Jean Viollet et al., *Eugénisme, stérilisation, leur valeur morale* (Paris: SPES, 1929). For background see Martine Sevegrand, "Limiter les naissances. Le cas de conscience des catholiques français (1880-1939)," *Vingtième siècle. Revue d'histoire* 30 (April-June 1991): 40-54; Martine Sevegrand, *Les enfants du bon Dieu: les catholiques français et la procréation au XXe siècle* (Paris: Albin Michel, 1995); Martine Sevegrand and Jean Viollet, *L'amour en toutes lettres: questions à l'abbé Viollet sur la sexualité, 1924-1943* (Paris: Albin Michel, 1996).

27. Dietrich von Hildebrand, *Reinheit und Jungfräulichkeit* (Munich: Kösel & Pustet, 1927); Dietrich von Hildebrand, *Die Ehe* (Munich: J. Müller, 1929).

28. Theresa Notare, "'A Revolution in Christian Morals': Lambeth 1930, Resolution #15: History and Reception" (Ph.D. diss., Catholic University of America, 2008).

29. Shaji George Kochuthara, *The Concept of Sexual Pleasure in the Catholic Moral Tradition* (Rome: Editrice Pontificia Università Gregoriana, 2007), 246-50.

30. See Abbé Jean Viollet: *Le mariage* (Tours: Mame, 1932); *La psychologie du mariage* (Paris: Association du mariage chrétien, 1935); *La loi chrétienne du mariage: prescriptions et défenses* (Paris: Éd. Mariage et Famille, 1936). See also Jean Viollet et al., *Où en sommes-nous?: La doctrine familiale de l'Église catholique et le problème du mariage dans les deux mondes* (Paris: Éditions Mariage et Famille, 1932).

extended title *Love and the Mystery of Sacramental Marriage*. The following year, a French translation of Herbert Doms's groundbreaking
(although somewhat unorthodox) *On the Meaning and End of Marriage* (1935) was published by Desclée de Brouwer.[31] In short, by the
time the Council opened twenty-five years later, discourse about modern companionate marriage had been going strong for at least four
decades.

As a corollary, the Council's indecisiveness on birth control may
have been eminently understandable in terms of the legalization of
Enovid-10 just five years earlier; but it is less so when seen within the
longer duration—and that duration was long indeed. Divorce laws
and birth limitation in the late nineteenth century were outgrowths
of urban mentalities: mass migrations of farmers to industrial centers
forged the new working classes while bourgeois capitalists moved to
the new "suburbs" ringing the great cities.[32] Even before the United
States entered the Great War, Margaret Sanger (an Irish Catholic
born in 1879) opened the first American birth control clinic in 1916
in defiance of the Comstock Act (1873). Leo XIII's *Arcanum* (1880)
had been a response to increasing agitation for the legalization of
divorce throughout Europe. The ability to end a marriage was, in turn,
a corollary of "companionate marriage." John Stuart Mill's *Subjection of
Women* (1869), appearing almost exactly one century before *Gaudium
et spes* and *Humanae vitae*—and published in perhaps the world's most
prosperous and powerful nation, presided over by Queen Victoria (a
female)—underscores the growing ferment. It was followed almost
immediately by the ill-fated and bloody Paris Commune (1871),
which, in its early utopian moments, embraced socialist ideals including gender equality.

Behind the nineteenth-century drama hovers the unnerving ghost

---

31. Dietrich von Hildebrand, *L'amour et le mystère du mariage sacramentel*,
trans. Benoît Lavaud (Fribourg, Switzerland: Fragnière Frères, 1936); Dietrich
von Hildebrand, *Le mariage* (Paris: Cerf, 1936); Herbert Doms, *Du sens et de
la fin du mariage*, trans. Marie-Simone Thisse and Paul Thisse, 2d ed. (Paris:
Desclée de Brouwer, 1937), orig. *Vom Sinn und Zweck der Ehe* (1935).

32. For an engaging overview, see *A History of Private Life*, vol. 4. *From the
Fires of Revolution to the Great War*, ed. Michelle Perrot; trans. Arthur Goldham-
mer (Cambridge, MA: Belknap Press of Harvard University Press, 1990).

of Olympe de Gouges, a specter haunting egalitarianism. Two years after "The Declaration of the Rights of Man and of the Citizen," de Gouges authored the *Declaration of the Rights of Woman and the Female Citizen* (1791), a riposte to the male revolutionaries who left women out of their universalizing project. The French Revolution eventually included the destruction of aristocratic and clerical privileges, Jewish emancipation, and religious freedom for Huguenots, the abolition of slavery, the legalization of divorce, and decriminalization of sodomy. And yet, curiously, the Revolution—deeply marked by gender anxieties—never did extend citizens' rights to women.[33] At age forty-five, de Gouges was guillotined (November 1793), one year after Mary Wollstonecraft's *A Vindication of the Rights of Woman* (1792). It has become a truism to say that, in Vatican II, the church finally came to terms with the French Revolution. This might be also true in an unintended way: like the Revolution, the Council came to terms with Enlightenment political ideals; but also like the Revolution, the Council resisted accommodating biopolitical ideals.

To say that the Council's lack of awareness of biopolitical issues was due to the sudden eruption of the sexual revolution in the 1960s is thus both true (insofar as that decade marked a decisive moment in producing the world in which we now live) and untrue (insofar as these issues had been percolating since at least the French Revolution[34]). Certainly, part of the reason that the Council was handicapped in addressing them is that it felt constrained by 1930s-1950s papal pronouncements still fresh in the memory (especially Pius XII's 1951 Allocution to Italian Midwives). By contrast, the magisterial teachings of the mid-nineteenth century—vitriolic opposition to democracy and suffrage, religious freedom, and other liberal political

---

33. Lynn Hunt, *The Family Romance of the French Revolution* (Berkeley: University of California Press, 1992); Lynn Hunt, ed., *Eroticism and the Body Politic* (Baltimore, MD: Johns Hopkins University Press, 1991).

34. Indeed, the birth rate in France began to drop significantly in the 1770s and 1780s just prior to the Revolution, suggesting that at least some citizens saw it as a means of improving their standard of living. See Roger Chartier, *The Cultural Origins of the French Revolution*, trans. Lydia G. Cochrane (Durham, NC: Duke University Press, 1991), 96-100; cf. Gareth Stedman Jones, *An End to Poverty?: A Historical Debate* (New York: Columbia University Press, 2004).

ideals—had largely disappeared from memory. More recent documents—like *Arcanum* (1880), *Casti connubii* (1930), and *Quadragesimo anno* (1931)—largely framed biopolitical issues in neoscholastic terms of sexual morality. (Indeed, the denial of "parvity of matter" by manualist theologians in cases of sexual issues—a catch-all distinction that disregarded the usual qualifications of intentionality and circumstances—made every deviation from the narrow norm a matter of "serious" sin.[35]) In other words, unlike political issues, biopolitical ones were specifically *not* framed in terms used by the broader culture—that is, a discourse about the extension and application of egalitarianism, individual rights, and self-determination to broader gender- and sexually-defined subjects.

Another part of the reason for the Council's lack of awareness or concern must surely be the fact that it was almost exclusively a gathering of celibate males. Perhaps for many Catholics this is such an accepted element of the cultural landscape as to be invisible: it requires the unnatural act of historical thinking to render visible the invisible.[36] The combination of celibate male participants' social location and their intellectual and discursive formation—again, largely neoscholastic and manualist thought throughout the twentieth century—provided (and hence circumscribed) the preconditions of possibility for what was thinkable. What questions could and would be raised? In what language and categories would they be framed? What would constitute valid modes of

---

35. "The moral theology manuals unanimously taught that in sexual sins there was no parvity of matter—in other words, every sexual sin, even if it is just an internal sin, always involves grave matter. . . . In a 1966 address to the Catholic Theology Society of America, Charles Curran disagreed with the position that no parvity of matter exists in sexual sin and applied this assertion specifically to masturbation." See Charles E. Curran, *Catholic Moral Theology in the United States: A History* (Washington, DC: Georgetown University Press, 2008), 192.

36. Samuel S. Wineburg, *Historical Thinking and Other Unnatural Acts: Charting the Future of Teaching the Past* (Philadelphia: Temple University Press, 2001). Compare Joan W. Scott: "Making visible the experience of a different group exposes the existence of repressive mechanisms, but not their inner workings or logics; we know that difference exists, but we don't understand it as relationally constituted. For that we need to attend to the historical processes that, through discourse, position subjects and produce their experiences"; see Scott, "The Evidence of Experience," *Critical Inquiry* 17.4 (Summer 1991): 773-97, at 779.

discourse and argument? A counterfactual history of the Council might fantasize about the perspectives the same gathering would have adopted had half of its members been celibate females, noncelibate males, noncelibate females, or any combination thereof.

Two further conciliar issues should be included under the broad umbrella of biopolitics and biopower: first, the exclusion of women religious from the Council's streamlined restatement of the church's hierarchical structure (and the consequent near disappearance of women's orders since then); and second, the recasting of the church as the "people of God" with explicit emphases on the dignity of the laity and the encouragement to turn to the laity for expertise.

It has become a cliché to say that women have never had power in the church. I suggest that this perception is a tragic aftereffect of the Council and a consequence of the fragility of memory. Although women had not been ordained, the church's labyrinthine structures had provided spaces for power acknowledged by both clergy and laity. However, *Lumen gentium* eliminated the days when bishops and even popes might seek the counsel and assistance of a Hildegard of Bingen or Catherine of Siena. In a thoroughly twentieth-century manner that was both ultramodernist and neoprimitivist, the Constitution on the Church aimed at *ressourcement*, leap-frogging over centuries in order to clear away cluttered accretions: abbots and abbesses, fathers and mothers general, monks and nuns, cloistered and anchoresses, regular, cathedral, and lay canons. Modernity aims at streamlined structure and efficiency, and the modernist Council recognized three categories of ordained celibate males that constitute the church's "hierarchical structure":

> Bishops, therefore, with their helpers, the priests and deacons, have taken up the service of the community, presiding in place of God over the flock, whose shepherds they are, as teachers for doctrine, priests for sacred worship, and ministers for governing. . . . Thus the divinely established ecclesiastical ministry is exercised on different levels by those who from antiquity have been called bishops, priests and deacons.[37]

---

37. *Lumen gentium*, 20, 28.

After nearly fifteen hundred years of being central to Catholicism's self-identity—indeed, among the first acts of Henry VIII's Reformation and the French Revolution had been the dissolution of monasteries—consecrated religious were relegated to an indeterminate borderland and vague vocation:

> From the point of view of the divine and hierarchical structure of the Church, the religious state of life is not an intermediate state between the clerical and lay states. . . . Thus, the state which is constituted by the profession of the evangelical counsels, *though it is not the hierarchical structure of the Church*, nevertheless, undeniably belongs to its life and holiness.[38]

This loss of identity for the religious life was certainly felt by both men and women. However, while male religious maintained the possibility of ordination and fitting into "ecclesiastical ministry," female religious did not.

Whatever the many causal factors, in a tragically short span of time, the everyday face of the church—which for most Catholics had been primarily a female face—has been largely erased from memory. Happily, historical research is stepping into memory's vacuum as scholars recover the lives of millions of women religious, especially the immigrant women who built the Catholic Church in America.[39]

---

38. *Lumen gentium*, 43, 44. Emphasis added.

39. Anne M. Butler, *Across God's Frontiers: Catholic Sisters in the American West, 1850-1920* (Chapel Hill: University of North Carolina Press, 2012); Kathleen Sprows Cummings, *New Women of the Old Faith: Gender and American Catholicism in the Progressive Era* (Chapel Hill: University of North Carolina Press, 2009); Karl Markus Kresi, *Lakotas, Black Robes, and Holy Women: German Reports from the Indian Missions in South Dakota, 1886-1900*, trans. Corinna Dally-Starna (Lincoln: University of Nebraska Press, 2007); Emily Clark, *Masterless Mistresses: The New Orleans Ursulines and the Development of a New World Society, 1727-1834* (Williamsburg, VA: Omohundro Institute of Early American History and Culture; Chapel Hill: University of North Carolina Press, 2007); Maureen Fitzgerald, *Habits of Compassion: Irish Catholic Nuns and the Origins of New York's Welfare System, 1830-1920* (Urbana: University of Illinois Press, 2006); Suellen M. Hoy, *Good Hearts: Catholic Sisters in Chicago's Past* (Urbana: University of Illinois Press, 2006); Bernadette McCauley, *Who Shall Take Care of Our Sick? Roman Catholic Sisters and the Development of Catholic Hospitals in New*

One historian comments on Margaret McGuinness's *Called to Serve: A History of Nuns in America* (2013):

> For generations of American Catholics, the face of their church was, quite literally, a woman's face—the nursing sister in the hospital where they were born, the teaching sister in the school where they were educated, the caring sister who helped them through times of trouble. McGuinness recovers the compelling story of these sisters and puts them back at the center of American Catholic history.[40]

Along with the rapid diminishment of women's congregations has been the erasure of their memory. This has resulted in a critically distorted image of the church, identified in both the official and popular imagination with its (celibate male) bishops and priests. The image has been underscored and crippled by the sexual abuse scandals of the recent past.

The problem is even more complex in considering the category "laity." *Lumen gentium* defined the category thus: "The term laity is here understood to mean all the faithful except those in holy orders and those in the state of religious life specially approved by the church.... What specifically characterizes the laity is their secular nature.... [T]he laity, by their very vocation, seek the kingdom of God by engaging in temporal affairs and by ordering them according to the plan of God."[41] The language is significant: the document distinguishes between "secular" and (implicitly) "sacred" natures. However, if read through a biopolitical lens, what remains unspoken and invisible is that "laity" denotes the noncelibate "other" of celibates, both (male) clergy and (male and female) vowed religious.

York City (Baltimore, MD: Johns Hopkins University Press, 2005); Carol K. Coburn and Martha Smith, *Spirited Lives: How Nuns Shaped Catholic Culture and American Life, 1836-1920* (Chapel Hill: University of North Carolina Press, 1999). Cf. the presently unpublished documentary film by Bren Ortega Murphy, "A Question of Habit" (2010). See www.questionofhabit.com.

40. James M. O'Toole, jacket endorsement for Margaret M. McGuinness, *Called to Serve: A History of Nuns in America* (New York: New York University Press, 2013).

41. *Lumen gentium*, 31.

At least in theory, the Council effected a revolution in thought when it recovered the vocation of the laity thanks (in Paul Lakeland's words) to "overcoming baptismal amnesia." Moreover, the Council emphasized that the church's clerical authorities cannot be expected to have all the answers.

> Secular duties and activities belong properly although not exclusively to laymen. Therefore acting as citizens in the world, whether individually or socially, they will keep the laws proper to each discipline, and labor to equip themselves with a genuine expertise in their various fields. . . . Let the layman not imagine that his pastors are always such experts, that to every problem which arises, however complicated, they can readily give him a concrete solution, or even that such is their mission. Rather, enlightened by Christian wisdom and giving close attention to the teaching authority of the Church, let the layman take on his own distinctive role.[42]

The teaching church would rely on the expertise possessed by the "laity"—the 1960s era of *Mad Men* probably intended the specific designation of lay *men*—in order to solve new dilemmas. In theory, it seemed as though a new day had dawned.

In fact, however, the church after the Council found itself in a Catch-22. On the one hand, newly emergent issues were biopolitical ones, life processes as the contested objects of politics and power: divorce and remarriage; contraception; abortion; same-sex relationships. These were issues about which the "laity"—meaning not merely "nonclerics" but (as a biopolitical category) "noncelibates"—would presumably have had some direct experience (and perhaps expertise). On the other hand, it is precisely with respect to these issues that the church seemed to reserve ultimate judgment to its own hierarchical members (by definition, celibate males), ultimate interpretative categories (e.g., sexual morality as opposed to individual rights), and authority. This Catch-22 ended up in the "credibility gap" identified by Margaret Farley.[43] The exemplar of this dynamic was the process

---

42. *Gaudium et spes*, 43.

43. "But there is an even more serious reason . . . for a lack of credibility regard-

leading to the promulgation of *Humanae vitae*. Pope Paul VI had gathered together a diverse group of theologians, biologists, medical doctors, psychiatrists, and married couples: a large consultative body equipped (again quoting *Gaudium et spes*) "with a genuine expertise in their various fields." In the end the pontiff rejected their recommendations and launched the encyclical into the hot summer of '68.

The final result is the paradox unveiled by looking at the Council as a fulcrum poised between two epochs: coming out of the earlier political epoch, the Council encouraged a turn to "laity" with expertise in matters political and scientific—just as it had learned to do in the cases of heliocentrism, evolution, democracy, and religious liberty. However, looking ahead to the imminent epoch marked by biopolitics, the Council's counsel was set aside as the church retreated and reclaimed for itself ultimate authority on the "life" issues about to erupt for the "laity"—contraception, abortion, same-sex relationships, divorce, and remarriage. Much of the time since 1968 has been spent trying to reconcile the everyday lives of noncelibate "laity" with a magisterial authority reserved to celibate males.

* * * * *

As I write this in January 2014, Pope Francis has effected a small revolution during his short time in office since March 2013. At the end of July 2013, the pope spoke to the leadership of the Episcopal Conferences of Latin America (CELAM) and posed rhetorical challenges:

> In practice, do we make the lay faithful sharers in the Mission? Do we offer them the word of God and the sacraments with a clear awareness and conviction that the Holy Spirit makes himself manifest in them?
>
> As pastors, bishops and priests, are we conscious and convinced of the mission of the lay faithful and do we give them the freedom to continue discerning, in a way befitting their growth as disciples, the mission which the Lord has entrusted to them? Do we support them and accompany them, overcoming the

---

ing the Church's opposition to abortion. This is the less than happy record of the Church in relation to women." See Farley, "Church in the Public Forum," 91.

temptation to manipulate them or infantilize them? Are we constantly open to letting ourselves be challenged in our efforts to advance the good of the Church and her mission in the world?[44]

Two months later, on September 21 (the six-month anniversary of his election), Francis's first interview was simultaneously published in multiple translations. His remarks extended those earlier ones concerned with infantilizing the faithful. Reading Vatican I's definition of "that infallibility with which the Divine Redeemer willed that his Church should be endowed" through the lens of both *Lumen gentium* (people of God; *infallibilitas in credendo*) and *Gaudium et spes* (joys and sorrows), Francis echoed Paul VI's image of the church as "the pilgrim People of God":

> The people itself constitutes a subject. And the church is the people of God on the journey through history, with joys and sorrows. Thinking with the church, therefore, is my way of being a part of the people. And all the faithful, considered as a whole, are infallible in matters of belief, and the people display this *infallibilitas in credendo*, this infallibility in believing, through a supernatural sense of the faith of all the people walking together.[45]

The pope continued: "We cannot insist only on issues related to abortion, gay marriage and the use of contraceptive methods. This is not possible.... The church's pastoral ministry cannot be obsessed with the transmission of a disjointed multitude of doctrines to be imposed insistently."[46] This excessive public discourse, suggested the pope, has been detrimental to the church's moral authority. It has had the unintended effect of erasing or silencing the church's advocacy for

---

44. Pope Francis, "Address to the Leadership of the Episcopal Conferences of Latin America during the General Coordination Meeting," Sumaré Study Center, Rio de Janeiro (Sunday, July 28, 2013), paragraphs 3.3 and 3.5; Vatican website.

45. Antonio Spadaro, S.J., and Pope Francis, "A Big Heart Open to God," *America* (September 30, 2013): 15-38, at 22. See Paul VI, *Solemni hac liturgia* (*Credo of the People of God*), June 30, 1968. For Vatican I, see Denzinger-Schonmetzer, *Enchiridion symbolorum* 3074; for *infallibilitas in credendo*, see *Lumen gentium*, 12.

46. Spadaro and Pope Francis, "A Big Heart," 26.

numerous other issues including global poverty, lack of food, abuses of human rights, and care for the environment—issues that were close to the hearts of his immediate predecessors as well.[47]

In late 2013 and early 2014, Pope Francis has referenced at least three concerns of the politics of life:

1. Francis has called for an extraordinary synod on "Pastoral Challenges of the Family in the Context of Evangelization" to be held in October 2014. In an unprecedented move intended to solicit expertise from the laity, preparation for the synod included a questionnaire sent throughout the world. (Cooperation with and resistance to this directive varied between nations and even dioceses during the late fall of 2013.) Among other issues, the pope has called for the synod to consider a "somewhat deeper pastoral care of marriage," including the reception of communion by divorced and remarried Catholics.
2. On January 24, 2014, the Vatican spokesman confirmed that Francis is working on an encyclical that will concern "ecology" and specifically the "ecology of man."
3. On January 25, 2014, in an address to the Centro Italiano Femminile, Francis envisioned a "more capillary and incisive" role for women in the church, including those venues in which "the most important decisions are adopted."

While the ultimate results of these initiatives cannot be known as I write, the post-1968 stalemate detailed in this chapter does not seem as frozen this January 2014 as it was twelve months ago.

* * * * *

I conclude by returning to the words "biopolitics" and "biopower." Just about three decades ago, historian Joan Scott shook the academy with her article modestly entitled "Gender: A Useful Category of Historical Analysis."[48] Since then, "gender" has joined the other two overarching

---

47. Compare Farley: "Preoccupation with abortion has overshadowed all other issues important to the Church's political agenda." See Farley, "Church in the Public Forum," 90.

48. Joan W. Scott, "Gender: A Useful Category of Historical Analysis," *The American Historical Review*, 91.5 (December 1986): 1053-75.

scholarly categories of class and race in order to form the triumvirate of nineteenth- and twentieth-century historical research. I would like to make a more modest suggestion: at the very least, "biopolitics" is a "useful" category of analysis for interpreting Vatican II and its aftermath.

Distinguishing between "politics" and "biopolitics" helps explain why the same Council can seem exhilarating in style and even prophetic at some moments while being unprepared and even oblivious at others. "Biopolitics" as a useful category can assist in studying and talking about issues in the everyday lived experience of nineteenth- and twentieth-century people without immediately framing these issues (as is the Catholic habit) in terms of moral theology and doctrine, a move that immediately severs linkages to the wider culture. If issues of reproduction, same-sex relationships, and stem cells continue to be seen only as "moral" issues in ways that an earlier epoch's storms over democracy, religious liberty, and Jewish dignity are not—ironically, a present-day application of the manualist conviction that "parvity of matter" holds for politics but not biopolitics—then historical parallels and possible understanding will be obfuscated. Finally, the category of "biopolitics," precisely because it considers "life" as a broad spectrum stretching from the microbe to the planet, is able to transcend and unify—and thereby offer unexpected insights on—topics usually considered within more limited purviews: gender, sexuality, race, eugenics, marriage and family, celibacy, reproduction, medical technology, end-of-life, global population, environmental studies, and so on.

The years 1962-1965 stand as a fulcrum. When we look at December 1965 from the political vantage point, the Council appears to have concluded an armistice with modernity. However, looking at the same moment from the biopolitical perspective, the Council seems to have been caught off guard, struggling to keep up with rapid currents outstripping its capacity to make sense. One way of historically interpreting this seeming paradox is that biopolitical issues in 1965 had taken over the recently vacated spaces once occupied by eighteenth- and nineteenth-century political issues. Even as the Council euphorically celebrated its peace with the past, it unknowingly danced on the edge of a volcano.

2

Women and Vatican II
Theological Excavations and Soundings

SALLY VANCE-TREMBATH

This essay is a theological mining expedition. The Council has rich treasures for women in the church, but we shall not find them on the surface level. The key to interpreting Vatican II is the reimagined theological anthropology that animated the Council's most creative teachings.[1] The gems of theology that offer hope for women are not located by identifying selections from the documents about women and then describing how they have or have not been taught effectively. We shall instead have to excavate the Council itself, as a whole, rather than simply its published texts. The Council was an event that recalibrated the notion of the human person in order to engage modern intellectual discourse, especially the global context and modern understandings of the human search for knowledge.

As in many things Catholic, the genius of Vatican II resides more in its method than in its texts. To do this we will follow Karl Rahner's summary of the Council as the beginning of the church's "third phase of existence."[2] Extending our excavation analogy, the unity of the human and the divine that is proclaimed in the Christian church is the mother lode of theological reflection. It is the richest vein that

---

1. Gustav Thils, "En pleine fidélité au Concile du Vatican II," *La Foi et le temps* 10 (1980): 278. See also Gustave Thils, "Trois traits caractéristiques de l'Église postconciliare," *Bulletin de théologie africaine* 3 (1981): 233-45.

2. Karl Rahner, "Basic Theological Interpretation of the Second Vatican Council," in *Concern for the Church: Theological Investigations, vol. XX*, trans. Edward Quinn (New York: Crossroad, 1986), 82-84.

animates the church's work for Jesus' mission. Rahner claims, though, that this vein had accumulated the silt of Western and especially European thought forms during the period from the so-called Council of Jerusalem until Vatican II.[3] The theological reflection that had been so flexible and adaptable during that period was not sufficient to deal with the "new world" that began to emerge in the twentieth century. By uncovering this bedrock, we shall see features of this theological anthropology that are ready for application to the concerns of women. We shall excavate two sites from the Council that demonstrate the way Vatican II applied this bedrock notion of the human person to specific theological, ecclesial challenges. After we do this, we will then move to explore a third site: the emerging church under the leadership of Pope Francis.

Identifying tactics that were successful is the first step toward applying those tactics to the concerns of women. The first site where Vatican II cleared away the accumulations of the previous ecclesiological period is its response to groups that had been oppressed and marginalized by the institutional church. I shall explore this vein with tools from feminist discourse. The second site is the Council's use of the ancient principle *lex orandi, lex credendi*. The application of this principle is one of the essential features of Vatican II. The Council's use of it is a signal mark of the progressive trajectory that made Vatican II a transformative event.[4] Our working translation is "the way we pray displays what we believe." This principle is axial; both sides influence each other. For these two sites, we only need probe their depth. Our third site, though, is just coming into view, and so here we will take exploratory soundings. That site is the pontificate of Francis. Borrowing further from this mining metaphor, let us note that before miners dig, they take soundings and listen for indications of useful and plentiful sediments. There is a promising field that has emerged as

---

3. Ibid.

4. There are many studies that argue thus. Two representative ones are Bernard Botte, *From Silence to Participation: An Insider's View of Liturgical Renewal*, trans. John Sullivan (Washington, DC: Pastoral Press, 1988); and Hans Küng and David Tracy, eds., *Paradigm Change in Theology: A Symposium for the Future*, trans. Margaret Köhl (New York: Crossroad, 1989).

a possible new vein, perhaps even a mother lode in the early ministry of Francis. There are early signs that he is deliberately implementing Vatican II's methods in the way that he is exercising the papal office. If so, that may be the best "news" that Catholic women have heard in a long time.

Preliminary Remarks

When I am asked to speak about Vatican II, I usually begin my remarks by describing the Council documents as some of the best-kept secrets in the Catholic tradition. Even a small taste of these rich documents is invigorating. The energy generated often leads to frustrated questions about why the Council's teachings have not been applied to women. Those questions, in turn, often animate a desire for a "Vatican III." When asked when there will be such a Council, however, my answer is always the same: women do not need Vatican III because Vatican II launched the requisite paradigm shift. In the nature of the case, such shifts are rare and infrequent; hence their importance. Vatican II provided us with all the theological reflection we need to navigate the changes our era has brought and continues to bring.

The challenge that paradigm shifts present, in contrast to the regular growth and development of an established framework, is the disorientation that accompanies the creativity presupposed by them. The trick lies in stabilizing the new framework by actually implementing and using it. That stabilization has happened in many sectors of Catholic practice and theology. Where women are involved, however, large gaps remain between Vatican II's contribution and the actual treatment of women in the church. Profound teaching means little unless and until it becomes part of belief and practice in the church's life; that insight is distilled in the profundity of *lex orandi, lex credendi*. The ecclesiological principle of reception reminds us that teaching must be fashioned into actual processes and practices. Women do not need more words on women's roles in the church. Women need leaders to create a church where competent and well-trained women can exercise leadership. We need a church where women no longer have to do the ecclesial equivalent of "work arounds" in order to fulfill their baptismal mission and often vocation. The good news for women is that the most challenging theological work has already been done. The theological anthropology of the Council is ready and waiting to be forged into new ways of being church that allow women to fully exercise their baptismal commitments.

What are the distinctive features of this theological anthropology? The first feature is a retrieval of the principle of sacramentality with regard to the human person. This principle describes the characteristically Catholic notion of how the divine is available and related to the human. The principle states that "all reality is potentially and in fact the bearer of God's presence and the instrument of divine action on our behalf."[5] This understanding of the unity of the human and the divine provides Catholic theology and practice with a stable foundation so that even during periods when theology is not at its conceptual best, this sacramental principle inoculates the church and provides protection from destructive forces.[6] Each of our theological sites contains veins of this bedrock principle. Sacramentality requires a balance between the divine and the human; the unity is neither oversupernaturalized and thus distanced from finite, contingent reality, nor overly domesticated and thus easily identified with and/or reduced to rubrics and rules. Sacramentality points to the intersection of the finite and the infinite. The finite is saturated with God's presence, but it is not overwhelmed with divine presence in ways that make the human disappear. The theological anthropology during the period just prior to Vatican II often tended toward magic, where the contingent reality was imbued with more supernatural power than it possessed. For example, neo-Platonism's characterization of human rationality sometimes became so identified with divine activity (*excessus*) that by default it identified the less rational features of human character as more animalistic and thus more distant from God. When applied to women this is particularly challenging because of the relentless tendency to define women in terms of their biological capacity for motherhood. According to this reasoning, women are seen as less rational and thus less connected to the divine. This overphysicalizing of the way the human is connected to the divine was

---

5. Richard P. McBrien, *Catholicism: Completely Revised and Updated* (San Francisco: HarperCollins, 1994), 1250.

6. Ibid.

deconstructed at Vatican II by turning to the transcendental features of the human person as such. A deeper excavation of these ideas follows.

Site One: Excavating the Council's Treatment of Oppressed Groups

Our first excavation site comes from resistance movements. Since our particular excavation seeks hope for women in the church, we begin with the feminist tactic of "talking back," whereby oppressed groups reject the names given to them by their oppressors. Resistance scholars claim that this is the first step out of oppression. "Talking back" transforms the oppressed by allowing them to name themselves. This sharpens the lines of the other features that come along with names. It begins the process of self-description as well. Most descriptions of women in the church were formulated by males with little or no consideration of the lived experience of women. Indeed, women were not asked to describe themselves. "Talking back" refuses to answer to names that oppress. Resistance figure Audre Lorde tells us, "The master's tools will never dismantle the master's house."[7] Women will begin to flourish in the church once we have "dismantled" oppressive descriptions of women. Women are currently described not as full human persons but instead are viewed with reference to men as the norm or starting point. In contrast to this, women see themselves as full human persons rather than a truncated version of a male. Feminist scholar bell hooks defines "talking back" as "speaking as an equal to an authority figure."[8] Women need to "talk back" to the institutional church. Any authority that the institutional church has flows from the gospel. The gospel recognizes that women and men are persons identically animated by the indwelling presence of God's Holy Spirit. If women "talk back" as equals, they execute both transformative and reformative work. Vatican II's theological anthropology authorizes and enables this "talking back."

Although Vatican II happened when resistance scholarship was in its infancy, the Council did perform its own version of "talking

---

7. Audre Lorde, *Sister Outsider*, Crossing Press Feminist Series (Freedom, CA: Ten Speed Press, 1984), 112.

8. bell hooks, *Talking Back* (Boston, MA: South End Press, 1989), 32.

back." The Council explicitly reconfigured the church's toxic relationship with several oppressed groups. The Council "talked back" to
itself, as it were, with the intention of transforming and reforming its
previous relationships with other groups and cultures. For instance,
Nostra aetate "talked back" to anti-Semitism—its own as well as the
larger culture's. The Jews are not "rejected, accursed or perfidious," but
instead, Christians and Jews alike share "a common spiritual heritage."
Unitatis redintegratio "talked back" to anti-Protestant impulses. Protestants, Orthodox, and Anglicans are not "heretics and schismatics" but
companion Christians in their own churches or ecclesial communities.
Dignitatis humanae "talked back" to an oppressive notion of religious
freedom that protected only Catholic practice. Vatican II declared that
religious freedom does not flow from Catholic membership but from
the constitutive dignity of human persons themselves, including persons who reject institutional religion. *Sacrosanctum concilium* "talked
back" to shrunken notions of grace and sacramental action. The sacraments are not for dispensing a commodity but rather invite "the full,
conscious and active participation" of the whole assembly. In *Lumen
gentium* the Council "talked back" to a name like "the perfect society"
that collapsed the Reign of God into the structures of the institutional
church. *Lumen gentium* rejected names that were fashioned with little
or no attention to the deepest identity of the church. In the Council's
view the church is not the Reign of God in institutional form; it is
the assembly animated by God's in-dwelling presence that serves the
historic mission of Jesus Christ.[9]

"Talking back" is essential in order for women to be recognized
as fully human baptized persons and able to function as such in the
church. The current bureaucratic system gives itself a greater status
than the status of a female baptized person. "Talking back" is one
strategy for drilling down to the sacramental bedrock of the Catholic
tradition. "Talking back" identifies the weak or nonexistent sacramentality upon which most of the current teaching about women rests.
Women need a theological language of resistance that implements the
theological anthropology of the Council. What would such a language
look like? How might we take the measure of names to identify those

---

9. McBrien, *Catholicism*, 723.

that oppress and those that give life? Another transformative council of the church provides a template.

At Chalcedon, the early church rejected notions of Jesus Christ that undermined the unity of the human and the divine in his person and mission. By crafting the Chalcedonian formulation of the Incarnation from the bedrock principle of sacramentality—and methodologically from *lex orandi, lex credendi*—that Council "talked back" and rejected descriptions of Jesus that diminished his humanity as well as notions that portrayed him as a divine being masquerading as a man. Today we need such a Chalcedonian formula for Vatican II's understanding of the human person. That formula has helped the church to dismantle many an anti-Christian "house." Women need tools like this to dismantle the oppressive features of the docetic, clerical house that masquerades as the full expression of God's church.

I have such a tool to suggest. The best tools are designed for specific tasks, and this one is designed expressly for the implementation of the rich teaching of Vatican II. I propose a category called "sacramental valence." In chemistry a valence indicates the capacity that allows one chemical to react with others. The valence of a particular element will determine the *way* it bonds with other elements. The Latin root of valence means "capacity," which is why its verbal form means "to be strong." The category provides a way to bond the Council's understanding of the church with its understanding of the human person. When persons in the church are described with a robust sacramental valence, they will readily connect with the church's identity and mission. We might even visualize the church as the rudimentary image of the atom with electrons swirling around a nucleus of neutrons and protons. The church is the dynamic expression of Jesus Christ, and his gospel is the work of his Father and the mission of their Holy Spirit. We need to be able to express the theological anthropology of the Council in dialogue with the way we understand the dynamism of the church. An understanding of the human person with an appropriate sacramental valence will coherently account for, and unite with, all the central truth claims of Christianity. Currently, the church's descriptions of women do not reflect such a valence. Instead, their identity is so overphysicalized that an imbalance is inevitably created between the human and the divine.

Were we to apply this notion of sacramental valence where would we find the weakest bonds? In the American context especially it is in the professional status of women in the church. Women already execute the vast majority of the person hours required by the church's commitment to the gospel. Women have plenty of ecclesial, gospel work. What they do not have is secure employment; proper access to, or funding for, training; processes and procedures that protect them; and they rarely have any institutional power. In sum, women are not treated as professionals in the institutional church even though the mission of that church would grind to a halt were their labor subtracted from it. This treatment is currently rooted in an understanding of women that begins with their capacity for motherhood rather than their capacity as persons who are receptive to and responsible for God's divine invitation. This understanding of women interferes with seeing women as professionals. This weak valence occurs in complete contrast to men, whose capacity for fatherhood is not seen as a constitutive feature of their identity. Hence, male parenthood is not seen as an obstacle to or denial of their spiritual "calling" as it is with women. Such a weakened sacramental valence makes women unavailable for many forms of ministry in the church, and thus harms the mission of that church.

American women could enlist other lessons from the history of resistance. There are models for resisting weak sacramental valences in the church's descriptions of women in the church. Sojourner Truth is an early heroine in resistance. Sojourner Truth is famous for her ringing question, "Ain't I a woman?"[10] before the Women's Rights Convention in Akron, Ohio, in 1851. She continued, "When that little black man in there, he says women can't have as much rights as men 'cuz Christ wasn't a women. Whar did your Christ come from? Whar did your Christ come from? From God and a woman. Man had nothing to do with him!"[11] As a member of an oppressed group, she rejects the identity given to her by others and claims her own. She made the clarion call that refused to be named by others. She "talked back." The

10. Suzanne Pullon Fitch and Roseann M. Mandziuk, *Sojourner Truth as Orator: Wit, Story, and Song* (Westport, CT: Greenwood Press, 1997), 103-8.

11. Ibid.

Council "talked back" over and over in texts of resistance that charted a new path forward. Now Catholic women need to "talk back." In addition to what has already been said, how else might we do that?

First, suppose we stop talking about *women* in the church. That starting point already presupposes a constitutive difference between baptized members of the church. But baptism does not allow for such a constitutive difference, a difference at the level of being. All members of the church are human persons made in the image and likeness of God, and hence they all share the same sacramental valence. Women will have a better future in the church when we no longer see book chapters entitled "Women in the Church." Women look for the time when we talk about people in the church and everyone knows that the reference is to baptized persons rather than male persons.

Second, let us "talk back" to the so-called theology of the body. The ideas that are clustered into this category come primarily from a long series of addresses given by Pope John Paul II. As authoritative as papal pronouncements are, they do not rise to the level of conciliar teaching. These talks presuppose an understanding of gender that cannot engage many of the experiences of actual women and men as they come to understand their own bodies. We have to "talk back" to theologies that use biology to determine human identity. Describing women with an overemphasis on biological and physical features leads to definitions of women with weak and even negative sacramental valences. Certainly the contingent realities of our bodies are involved in our identity, but to locate the mystery—the essence—of the human person in such structures mistakes mystery for magic. Magic assigns a power that a thing or person does not possess. The divine does saturate the human but as sacrament and not as an impersonal power. *Female* persons will not flourish in the church until they are first and fundamentally perceived as *baptized* persons.

Earlier I referred to various identities that the Council rejected. The most important of these is akin to women rejecting names that locate their gifts essentially in gender categories. "Talking back" does not end the discussion; it simply starts it at its true beginning. Vatican II did not resolve all Jewish-Christian issues; it simply located the mine shaft where these resolutions lay hidden. The church demanded a similar new starting point for descriptions of its nature and mission.

The Council rejected an institutional starting point. It rejected features of a previous identity in order to generate a new one. Perhaps the best way to apply Vatican II to women's needs has little to do with anything the Council explicitly said about women. What the Council said about the church itself is all that is needed for women to accept and act upon their own sacramental spirituality. It would make a profound and far-reaching difference for women if women made a similar move about their own nature and mission.

Site Two: The Use of *Lex orandi,* *lex credendi* at Vatican II

Having "talked back" theologically, let us now "talk back" liturgically. In so doing we follow another tactic used at Vatican II. Using the new understanding of the human person, the Council crafted new liturgical forms in order to express and implement this creative theology at the concrete level of corporate worship. Both moves reflected, and hence created, robust sacramental valences. The genius of this principle is how it uses an application or expression of a conceptual teaching to draw out the features of that teaching. When the Council members gathered for Eucharist in the non-Roman rites, it opened up the conceptual and theological space to perceive how the Tridentine rite itself had begun to display just the kind of weak sacramental valence we have been describing. I propose that we develop this principle into a new axiom that we can explicitly apply to all believers, both men and women, in the church: *Lex docendi, lex credendi,* roughly translated as "if you educate them you presuppose their capacity to be educated." This principle is rooted in the church's long commitment to the education of young women. The fact that we offer young women professional education affirms that they can execute the professions that require it. Providing women education, especially university-level education, presumes that they are full, human persons. The fact that they are not held to a different educational process or standard is proof positive that they could fulfill the same professions as identically educated males. If they can be educated by the church, then they must be able to hold any position for which that education already qualifies identically trained men.

Recently I have been teaching young women who are candidates for the Master's of Divinity. One of these deeply committed Catholic women repeatedly asks, what is this degree training me to do? Who will hire me? In any other discipline, women with graduate degrees in business, nursing, medicine, or education can look forward to employment. This is not so straightforwardly the case for women with professional degrees in Catholic theology. Add to that the other wrinkle, which is that most M.Div. programs continue to be shaped by the seminary model of training candidates for ordination. Our new axiom should therefore also be applied to undergraduate education. If we are going to educate young women in our Catholic universities then we should be creating the professional opportunities for them that such an education expects, in fact promises.

Hope for women lies in creating a church using the rich ore from Vatican II to forge material that will support the Council's vision. The church needs a new superstructure in order to become the church envisioned at the Council. Some of the foundation has been poured; we have yet to dismantle the rocky previous structure. This dismantling is necessary before we frame-in the new.

Site Three: Taking Soundings:
The Pontificate of Francis

The way Pope Francis has exercised his ministry indicates that his pontificate is another rich source of material for our new church. The initial soundings are positive. The first signal is his understanding of the ecclesial power of his actions. He may have out-gestured the champion of the *bella figura*, Pope John XXIII, by paying his own bills and rejecting so many creaturely comforts. This is good news for all Catholics; it might be especially good news for women. In addition, his *Evangelii gaudium* echoes significant speeches and texts from his two most reform-minded predecessors, Pope John XXIII and Pope Paul VI. I think it no accident that he strikes familiar chords. For example, the current bishop of Rome makes use of long-standing Catholic teaching about poverty and the just distribution of the world's goods. He does so primarily by drawing on teaching from previous texts. Is not everything Pope Francis says about economic justice something that Pope

Paul VI told us decades ago? *Evangelii gaudium* returns again and again to Pope Paul's richest text about the church. Could it be that while Pope John Paul II *took* the names of the popes of the Great Council, it is Francis who will finally *embrace* them and *implement* their vision? Many theologians and pastors and deeply faithful practicing Catholics rejected the moral reasoning of Pope Paul's *Humanae vitae*. The text that was intended to protect papal authority, undermined it. But that is not the saddest part of the story. The deepest sorrow for the church is the way that Pope Paul's voice was diminished. Pope Francis cites Pope Paul's masterpiece, *Evangelii nuntiandi*, repeatedly. *Evangelii nuntiandi* displays a robust sacramental valence by aligning the essence of the institutional church with the gospel. *Evangelii gaudium* sounds many of the same notes.

Our final sounding returns to the liturgical and appears grounded in Francis's Jesuit identity. Many people were excited by the first Jesuit pope because of the intellectual tradition of the Society of Jesus. The first soundings directed at the Jesuit features of Francis's methodology observe his preference for the liturgical before the conceptual. Pope Francis calls himself a sinner. He notes that the papacy needs conversion. The *lex orandi* of the sacrament of Reconciliation tells us that we must name sin and reject it. The institutional church needs to "go to confession." Indeed, let us get busy and perform the sacramental wisdom of naming the harm done to women by the diminished theological anthropology the church has used to name them. The power of Pope Francis's self-description lies not in any specific instance of harm. It lies in the profound recognition that ministry requires renewal and growth, and that movement involves naming the sin, repenting of it, and addressing the damage. Feminist scholarship of "talking back" is a kind of secular sacrament of reconciliation with particular emphasis on confession, naming sin, as necessary for describing reality. (Karl Rahner might call it an "anonymous sacrament.") Pope Francis's self-description is a sign of Ignatius's deep understanding of the freedom that comes once we recognize the character and shape of sinfulness in human existence. In the *Spiritual Exercises*, St. Ignatius recommends a general confession to close the first week of the process. Joseph Tetlow, an authority on spiritual direction, describes the wisdom of confession at the end of the First Week, which, for retreatants, involves "experiencing the reality of their sins. They have a keener insight during the Exercises into the malice and perversities of their sins. They appreciate more deeply the personal honor of Jesus Christ coming to them in Communion—which in turn confirms their courage to keep on in the interior life."[12] The papal ministry directed by such an interior life could indeed rebuild the church in the vision of Vatican II by paying as much attention to its theological presuppositions as to its published texts.

Is Pope Francis retrieving the voices of these pastoral and theological geniuses in order to rebuild the church with material they helped to forge? We have a few early points on a line. Let us hope and pray, with joy, that the line gets drawn.

---

12. Joseph A. Tetlow, S.J., *Choosing Christ in the World: A Handbook for Directing the Spiritual Exercises of St. Ignatius Loyola according to Annotations Eighteen and Nineteen* (Saint Louis, MO: Institute of Jesuit Sources, 1999), 211.

3

Another Legacy of Vatican II
Cultural Dilemmas among American Catholics

Jerome P. Baggett

Opening to Modern Culture and to Dilemmas Therein

If, more than a half-century ago, the election of a youthful and urbane Catholic president demonstrated to Catholics (and other Americans) that they no longer huddled behind the walls of a cultural fortress, the Second Vatican Council (1962-1965) told them this in explicitly theological language. Convened by seventy-seven-year-old and thus unlikely ecclesial reformer Pope John XXIII, Vatican II was intended to be, as he put it, an *aggiornamento*, an "updating" of the church. It was to be akin to opening the church's windows in order to allow the fresh air of contemporary thinking to breeze through its premodern edifice. This was precisely what happened. Truly an ecumenical Council, it was attended by more than twenty-six-hundred bishops and four hundred expert advisors from around the world, and news of its ongoing deliberations was broadcast to Catholics everywhere. What they discovered from hearing these reports, reading, or simply learning about the sixteen documents the bishops produced, as well as from the eventual implementation of changes those deliberations and documents proposed were new theological categories for conceptualizing their religion within a modern context.

As critical as Vatican II's changes were, they did not simply *cause* the transformation of American Catholicism that became so glaringly apparent in their aftermath. A better way to put it would be to say that

40

the Council provided American Catholics with an officially sanctioned language for comprehending and discussing the sociocultural changes so many of them were already experiencing. These new (or newly articulated) theological categories—a more egalitarian understanding of the church (the "people of God"), an emphasis on the inviolability of one's conscience (the person's "most sacred core and sanctuary"), an openness to the human and social sciences, to other cultures, to other faiths—made the faithful's entry into the cultural mainstream and ensuing embrace of modernity thinkable both for and as Catholics.

Moreover, encouraged by Vatican II to move beyond their aforementioned cultural fortress as well as the "Father-knows-best" kind of piety it safeguarded, American Catholics have since shown that they relate to their faith tradition in ways that people relate to culture more generally. Important lessons can be learned from this basic insight. For one thing, it is glaringly obvious that, for good or for ill, individual Catholics actively appropriate the religious scripts and meanings with which they are familiar. Both the remarkable variety among them and the religious changes that individual believers experience over the course of their lives indicate that they are not "cultural dopes."[1] They are not passive recipients of a religious culture that is simply planted in their brains and then directs their actions in essentially predictable ways. Rather, as sociologist Ann Swidler conceives it, cultures—and, critically, this includes religious traditions—are better understood as symbolic repertoires or "tool kits." Individuals actively select and make use of the symbolic tools therein based on what challenges they face, who they consider themselves to be, and which components they feel competent to utilize.[2]

A second lesson to keep in mind is that, as they actively engage in this interpretive process, Catholics necessarily alter their faith tradition somewhat. They appropriate some of its features, modify others, and reject still others in light of the needs and perspectives that coincide with the ever-shifting circumstances of their lives. As these

---

1. Harold Garfinkel, *Studies in Ethnomethodology* (Englewood Cliffs, NJ: Prentice-Hall, 1967), 68.

2. Ann Swidler, *Talk of Love: How Culture Matters* (Chicago: University of Chicago Press, 2001), chap. 2. See also her important article "Culture in Action: Symbols and Strategies," *American Sociological Review* 51 (1986): 273-86.

change, so too does their negotiation with tradition. They find themselves drawn to and conversant with some beliefs, some norms, and some symbols, whereas other beliefs, norms, and symbols no longer speak to them. Consequently, their tradition also changes in order to remain alive. After all, were answers to people's most capacious questions concerning what they hold sacred to be written in stone, then this would become that tradition's headstone—denoting not a living tradition but, instead, merely traditionalism's moribund truisms, quaint moralisms, and calcified doctrines.[3]

Lastly, as Catholics actively negotiate with their faith and as the tradition is reshaped (and revitalized) in the process, this engenders new cultural dilemmas as people attempt to go about the business of being both modern and Catholic. Unfortunately, these are seldom discussed. Certainly many observers have addressed specifically *institutional* dilemmas that have emerged since Vatican II and that are now part of the broader discourse on contemporary American Catholicism. Consider, for instance, what I will call the dilemma of institutional retention. Perhaps more than ever, Catholics are taught to practice openness toward faiths. Yet, at the same time, this partly accounts for roughly one in three of those Americans raised in the church eventually leaving. Comprising about one-tenth of the population, if "former Catholics" were considered a religious category, they would now be the nation's third largest.[4] Similarly, the post-Council decrease in the number of priests and religious sisters points to the dilemma of institutional leadership. Described as a "worst of both worlds" scenario, Vatican II's more egalitarian conception of church had the unintended consequence of reducing the benefits of entering religious life (e.g., high status, power) while maintaining its relatively high costs (e.g., celibacy, relative poverty), and this likely goes far in accounting for fewer Catholics entering the ranks of church leadership.[5]

---

3. In his classic *The Vindication of Tradition* (New Haven, CT: Yale University Press, 1984), Jaroslav Pelikan famously writes, "Tradition is the living faith of the dead, traditionalism is the dead faith of the living" (p. 65).

4. The Pew Forum on Religion and Public Life, *U.S. Religious Landscape Survey* (2008), chap. 2.

5. Laurence R. Iannaccone, "Why Strict Churches Are Strong," *American Journal of Sociology* 99 (1994): 1180-1211. See also Rodney Stark and Roger

Cultural dilemmas, however, are another matter altogether. These are unresolved questions that, ironically, are somewhat underwritten by the very theological categories and openness to the modern world endorsed by Vatican II. And they are true dilemmas in the sense that they are wrought of the ongoing process by which American Catholics negotiate with their faith tradition in order to align it with what they experience as true and, as a result, render it more relevant to their everyday lives. These dilemmas are less understood primarily because attending to them requires more in-depth observation than even our best survey data can provide. In an effort to address this problem, I undertook a more qualitative study of six very different parishes—rich and poor, urban and suburban, liberal and conservative, primarily white and comprised primarily of "minority" groups—in the San Francisco Bay area.[6] In addition to relying on both surveys and a few years of participant observation, my research assistants and I also did a lot of listening: We conducted approximately three hundred, two-hour interviews with active parishioners.

What I discovered during the course of this research and especially amid these conversations is that these parishioners have what social theorist Pierre Bourdieu calls "a feel for the game," a sense of how culture—in this case, Catholic culture—can be accessed, deployed, and improvised amid changing circumstances.[7] Like the basketball player who intuitively knows how to drive toward the basket even when faced with a configuration of players on the court he has never exactly seen before, having a feel for the symbols transmitted by the Catholic tradition is to have an intuitive sense of how to use them in innovative ways in novel situations. In short, when people have a feel for this particular game, it means they have attained the requisite cultural competence to negotiate with their religious tradition. Catholics acquire this by paying attention to how others live out their faiths. They also do it by

---

Finke, *Acts of Faith: Explaining the Human Side of Religion* (Berkeley: University of California Press, 2000), esp. chap. 7.

6. Jerome P. Baggett, *Sense of the Faithful: How American Catholics Live Their Faith* (New York: Oxford University Press, 2009).

7. Pierre Bourdieu, *The Logic of Practice*, trans. Richard Nice (Stanford, CA: Stanford University Press, 1990), 66.

taking stock of the things they hear others say, even when they might not agree with what has been said. They hear certain scripts again and again, and these help them to better consolidate and express their own identities as Catholics. Sometimes these can be as elaborated as accounts of what the Eucharist means to them or why it was (or was not) important for them to be married in the church. At other times, these can be seemingly simple phrases that, upon closer scrutiny, actually reveal key areas of identity negotiation. Like archeologists sifting through large bins of dirt to discover shards of pottery left by some ancient civilization, the careful sifter of discourse finds what I call conversational shards, which continually appear in Catholics' interactions with one another and represent important loci of cultural improvisation. Dusting off a few of these and examining them more closely should enable us to appreciate the subtle means by which Catholics attempt to live out their faith tradition as modern people and, in doing so, also engender for themselves (and their children) newfound, largely unresolved, cultural dilemmas.

"My Faith" and the Dilemma of Subjectivization

When parishioners describe themselves as Catholic, it is interesting to discover what they do not say. Rarely does one detect references to "Catholicism" (much less "Roman Catholicism") or to "the Catholic faith," or, as one would more likely hear in a religious studies classroom, to a "Catholic worldview." Rather, they say things like, "my faith is very important to me." Or they might confide that "I don't know where I'd be without my faith." After a bit of reflection, they might also say something akin to "my faith has really grown over the years," and, as one woman added wryly, "whether I've wanted it to or not!" This, they and so many others suggest, is not about systematic theology or magisterial teachings, or reciting the prayers correctly. It is about faith in things unseen, and, as the essential modifier "my" attests, it is also deeply personal.

What makes this conversational shard so ubiquitous among Catholics is the increasing degree of religious subjectivization that has occurred since about the middle of the past century. In other words, the locus of religious authority has rather dramatically shifted from what the renowned philosopher Immanuel Kant called "heterono-mous" authority—instantiated, for example, in religious leaders and theologians—to the individual self.[8] Increasing levels of educational attainment, the cultural revolution of the 1960s, the dissolution of tightly bound and religiously homogeneous communities: All these trends (and more, of course) are likely contributors to this cultural shift, which privileges questioning over obedience, journeying over steadfastness, and a commitment to personal growth and authenticity over collective adherence to objectified norms.

Importantly, while intuitively calibrated to this cultural shift, the "my faith" shard should not be written off as necessarily reflecting a "do your own thing" sensibility. This was surely not the case with Maria, a longtime catechism teacher at her parish. When asked about how she is different from her parents religiously, she is quite subtle in both deploying this conversational shard and touching upon other well-worn themes expressed by American Catholics today:

> Some might call me a "cafeteria Catholic," but I have to say that my faith is also deeply personal to me. I've grappled with it and come to terms with it in ways that make sense to me in ways it didn't before.
>
> *Do you ever question or doubt things the Church teaches?*
>
> Of course! I think you should always doubt because that gives you the drive to mature religiously. Questioning things keeps you from becoming passive, becoming like some kind of sheep. "Baa, baaaa!" That's not the sound of a spiritually alive person. We have to question in order to grow, and we have to grow if we want to be fully human.
>
> *Is that what being a religious person is all about?*
>
> I prefer to think of myself as more spiritual than religious.
>
> *What's the difference?*
>
> Well, even though I love the beauty of the mass and the Church's mystical tradition, and even though being a part of a larger community is so important to me, I think emphasizing

---

8. See Immanuel Kant, *Foundations of the Metaphysics of Morals*, trans. Lewis White Beck (1785; reprint, New York: Macmillan, 1990), 58-63.

spirituality means staying true to the core of Jesus' message and not to all the doctrinal trappings.... I think we all have to be on a faith journey because when people—and I include Church leaders here—when we realize how loved we are by God, then we'll love others in ways that far surpass what's outlined for us by doctrines. It's very intimate.

Notice all the cultural work Maria does. Hardly doing her own thing, she has seriously "grappled" with what she dubs "my faith." Moreover, she revalorizes the pejoratively intended moniker "Cafeteria Catholic" and appropriates it as an indicator of her own commitment to discernment. Not content to "pray, pay, and obey," as the old saw had it, she interrogates the tradition and selects those dimensions of it that resonate with her own experience—what is "deeply personal to me," "in ways that make sense to me," and so on. And she does something similar with Americans' mantra-like caveat, "I'm spiritual, but not religious." Often taken to signal a somewhat superficial faith, she draws upon it to signal her capacity to sift the wheat of what the philosopher William James once called "first-hand" religious experience from the chaff of her faith's less personally meaningful institutional dimensions.[9] Counterposed with spirituality's focus on the "core of Jesus' message," commitment to "love others," and on what is "very intimate" is, in her estimation, religion's "doctrinal trappings," "rules and regulations," and "what's outlined for us by the doctrines."

As laudable as this widespread emphasis on discernment and authenticity may be, it comes with a difficult dilemma. This can be summed up with a question: What does it mean to identify with an *authoritative* religious tradition? By "authoritative," I refer to the capacity to direct thought and action in ways distinguishable from the dictates of both the broader culture and self-interest. Concerning the former, when Catholics exercise their religious agency in the manner encapsulated by the "my faith" shard, this may appear to denote their pure autonomy independent of pressures from without. However, it is actually the manifestation of a deeply ingrained cultural expectation

---

9. William James, *The Varieties of Religious Experience* (New York: Macmillan, 1961).

that tells Catholics (and others) not only that they *can* make up their own minds when it comes to matters of faith, but also that they *must*. And, if the religious tradition is not authoritative in the sense of being independent of cultural expectations, nor does it bear the presumptive authority of being derived from community-based, rather than idiosyncratic, discernment. Whereas once traditions held communities together, individuals are now inclined to hold onto traditions on their own terms. Fair enough. Yet, when "my faith" exists alongside "his faith" and "her faith" and so forth, it becomes harder to think through either the place of "the Faith" in this scenario or the role played by the larger faith community in assessing (or perhaps trumping) one's own religious understanding.

"For Me" and the Dilemma of Religious Pluralism

The flipside of respecting others' perspectives is Catholics' reticence to universalize what is appealing, sensible, or true "for me." Because people typically perceive their faith as being so individualized, they tend to be reluctant to present their beliefs and commitments as necessarily applicable to others. "The Catholic religion is what's valid for me," "this is where, for me at least, God is present," "it's the best religion for me"—one hears this conversational shard with great frequency. "For me" seems to signify a widespread unwillingness to either judgmentally underestimate the validity of other people's truths or hubristically overestimate the validity of one's own.

This reticence has also been well documented as a prominent characteristic of contemporary American religion. When anthropologists Robert Lynd and Helen Lynd visited Muncie, Indiana (or "Middletown," as they pseudonymously called it), in the 1920s, they found that 94 percent of their respondents agreed that "Christianity is the one true religion, and all people should be converted to it."[10] However, when researchers returned to Muncie a little more than a half-century later, they were surprised to discover that, even though religious conviction and practice remained alive and well, only 41 percent of the

---

10. Robert S. Lynd and Helen Merrell Lynd, *Middletown: A Study in Modern American Culture* (1929; reprint, New York: Harcourt Brace Jovanovich, 1957), chap. 20.

city's inhabitants continued to agree with this statement.[11] Now this burgeoning inclusiveness is in full bloom across the American religious landscape. When asked in a recent national survey whether a "good person not of your faith can go to heaven," a whopping 93 percent of Catholics agreed.[12]

I got nary a whiff of the once-pervasive *extra ecclesiam nulla salus* [outside the Church there is no salvation] attitude among my interviewees. Instead, nearly everyone, even members of more conservative parishes, made use of the "for me" shard. A good example comes from my conversation with Richard, a member of his church's choir and a self-described "dyed-in-the-wool Catholic":

Do you think the Catholic faith is better or truer than other religious faiths?

To put it simply, I'd say Catholicism is the best religion for me.

Hmm. What do you mean by that exactly?

I think that if you have a relationship with God, it doesn't make any difference what you are. My feeling is that, based on what I know about the Tradition of the Church and its history, this is where I should be. But one of the things Isaiah says is that God's ways and man's ways are different. He makes that real clear. I don't know a lot about Hinduism and Buddhism but, as far as I can tell, they're synonymous with Christianity since they're about connecting to God and getting along with other people. And the same goes for Islam; it's about the same kind of basic principles.

Interesting. But, if that's the case, then why be specifically Catholic?

Because this is what works for me. It's the path that I think is working to make me closer to God. Besides, this is the Tradition I know and feel comfortable with.

---

11. Theodore Caplow, Howard M. Bahr, and Bruce A. Chadwick, *All Faithful People: Change and Continuity in Middletown's Religion* (Minneapolis: University of Minnesota Press, 1983), 91-55.

12. Robert D. Putnam and David E. Campbell, *American Grace: How Religion Divides and Unites Us* (New York: Simon & Schuster, 2010), 535.

As he suggests in mentioning Hinduism, Buddhism, and Islam, his "for me" signals a recasting of what it means to be Catholic within an increasingly pluralistic context. All of the parishioners in my study say they have acquaintances, coworkers, and close friends who adhere to different faiths or no faith. Almost all of them also have non-Catholic siblings, spouses, or children with whom they report having many meaningful conversations about all manner of religious topics. This daily exposure to religious pluralism generally does not make them "heteroglossic,"[13] that is, knowledgeably conversant in other religious traditions ("I don't know a lot about Hinduism and Buddhism," confides Richard). Rather, to coin a phrase, they are more "heterognostic" in the sense that they simply know about other denominations and religions; they have these faiths on their "radar screens," as it were.

As a consequence, they and other Catholics seem to have added what sociologist Alan Wolfe describes as an unofficial eleventh commandment for a growing number of Americans: "Thou shalt not judge."[14] What is more, "for me" also seems to denote their widespread uncertainty about religious matters. The parishioners I spoke to were remarkably forthcoming about this, and, rather than as an indication of their own ignorance, they tended to frame this theological humility in terms of their fuller appreciation of the utter inscrutability of God. So far, so good, one might suggest. However, the "for me" shard does present Catholics with a second dilemma: What does it mean to identify with a *particular* religious tradition? This is not at all obvious to Catholics today. Most of them flounder when trying to give a fuller account for what it would mean for their particular faith to be true in a more universal sense unbounded by the prevarications of their own subjectivities. Instead, like Richard, the majority of them link what they hold to be true to pragmatic ("what works for me") or affective ("feel comfortable with") justifications,

---

13. I borrow this term from Robert Wuthnow; see his *Christianity in the Twenty-First Century: Reflections on the Challenges Ahead* (New York: Oxford University Press, 1993), 108.

14. Alan Wolfe, *One Nation after All: What Middle-Class Americans Really Think about God, Country, Family, Racism, Welfare, Immigration, Homosexuality, Work, the Right, the Left, and Each Other* (New York: Viking, 1998), 54.

construals of which are eminently revisable and typically as fluid as are individuals themselves.

The "Good Person" and the Dilemma of Ethical Reductionism

The caveat "for me" reflects people's negotiation with the Catholic tradition by blunting its doctrinal edges. Another species of negotiation takes the focus off of doctrines altogether and places it upon the moral commitments derived from the church's teachings. This subtle exchange of religious "orthodoxy" (correct belief) for what some liberation theologians have called "orthopraxy" (correct action) as a way of defining oneself as Catholic has become commonplace.[15] Of course, the sacraments, the parish community, and comfort with the culture of Catholicism are important to people, and they cite these as key elements of their faith. Still, when queried about what best defines a good Catholic, parishioners almost unfailingly equate this with simply trying to be a "good person." Like the nonideological "Golden Rule Christians," whom sociologist Nancy Ammerman has found to increasingly populate American churches, Catholics are typically short on systematic theology and biblical scholarship and instead shift the weight of their religious identities more to the practice of everyday virtues.[16] Data for this is easy to come by. One recent national survey, for instance, presented Catholics with the statement "How a person lives is more important than whether he or she is Catholic" and discovered that the vast majority either strongly (55 percent) or somewhat (31 percent) agreed.[17]

Certainly Jeffrey, a Eucharistic minister at his parish, is in agreement. Somewhat after the point in our interview where I typically read and ask about various well-known Bible passages, such as the

---

15. See Leonardo Boff and Clodovis Boff, *Introducing Liberation Theology* (Maryknoll, NY: Orbis Books, 1989), 49-50.

16. Nancy T. Ammerman, "Golden Rule Christianity: Lived Religion in the American Mainstream," in *Lived Religion in America: Toward a History of Practice*, ed. David D. Hall (Princeton, NJ: Princeton University Press, 1997), 196-216.

17. William V. D'Antonio, Michele Dillon, and Mary L. Gautier, *American Catholics in Transition* (Lanham, MD: Rowman & Littlefield, 2013), 167.

famous Last Judgment passage in Matthew's Gospel, I inquired about how he understood what it means to be a good Catholic. Relying upon the broadly used "good person" shard, he responded:

> I would say that being a good Catholic in the traditional sense is going to Mass regularly, giving your time and money to the Church, praying regularly and embodying the beliefs of the Catholic religion in how you treat other people. I try to do that stuff. Overall, though, being a good Catholic is a goal that I'm trying to attain. And, since I don't know many of the fundamental doctrines of the religion, I mostly do this by trying to be a good person.
>
> *How does that relate to the Last Judgment passage* (Matthew 25:31-46) *I just read to you?*
>
> When I hear that passage, I'm reminded that we're called to do things for other people. I try to do that stuff, but it's a pretty daunting task. I wonder sometimes how good I have to be to be good.
>
> *How good do you have to be to be good?*
>
> Ahh, Jeez! I knew you'd ask that question! I don't think you have to be Mother Teresa good or anything. I think we're called to do those things in the story, but I don't think I have to do all of them now. I think the story is showing us the ideal and then we're supposed to grow toward that. I'm in process and that's the direction I'm hoping to grow spiritually.

There's a lot going on in this brief exchange. Rather than pointing to the fundamental doctrines of the faith, many of which he does not know, being a "good person" is central to his identity as a Catholic. Furthermore, living out his Catholicism in these terms has proven to be "pretty daunting," and, as such, it commits him to exerting considerable effort, evidenced by the four times he uses the verb "try." It also provides some direction for his life. Being a good person is a "goal" or an "ideal" to which he aspires; and, even though he's not (or perhaps not yet) "Mother Teresa good," he is still reasonably content with where he currently stands because he is "in process" and thus moving toward a better iteration of his present self.

Needless to say, there is generally much good that comes from trying to be a "good person," but there are also some dilemmas. An obvious one is that what constitutes the good person is loosely scripted in American culture. Definitions vary from one person to the next, and it can be fraught with uncertainty: "I sometime wonder," muses Jeffrey, "how good I have to be to be good." Still another, more pressing cultural dilemma reflected in the use of this shard can be posed: What does it mean to identify with a specifically *religious* tradition? When religious conviction gets reduced to living ethically, then it can seem wholly expendable upon observing the plethora of nonreligious paths toward goodness.[18] The religious dimension can thus get lost as Americans, Catholics included, increasingly come to realize that people can indeed be—to quote the title of a book written by Harvard University's humanist chaplain—"good without God."[19]

New Thoughts for a New Situation

Fifty years ago, the Second Vatican Council provided the faithful with new idioms that enabled them to think through their identities as both Catholic and modern. As American Catholics began to undertake this project of both/and-ness and as the culture of modernity went from being something "out there" to being very much "in here," they also found themselves in a new social situation that has required them to negotiate with their tradition such that it continues to resonate with their lived experience. This, in turn, has presented them with new cultural dilemmas. What does it mean today to live in accordance with an *authoritative* religious tradition when the triumphant Subject reigns supreme? To live according to a *particular* religious tradition within a pluralistic context populated by religious "others"? According to a specifically *religious* tradition when goodness springs from so many wells? These are difficult questions. And, without doubt, the Catholics with

---

18. For important scholarly treatments of this theme, see James Turner, *Without God, Without Creed: The Origins of Unbelief in America* (Baltimore, MD: Johns Hopkins University Press, 1985); and Charles Taylor, *A Secular Age* (Cambridge, MA: Harvard University Press, 2007).

19. Greg M. Epstein, *Good without God: What a Billion Nonreligious People Do Believe* (New York: William Morrow, 2009).

whom I have spoken have a very difficult time arriving at any answer to these questions for either themselves or their children.

The conservative backlash that came in the decades after Vatican II has not put this genie back in the bottle. Nor do I suspect that the pastoral sensitivities and renewed openness of the current pope, while generating enthusiasm among many, will alone suffice to resolve these dilemmas. Another fifty years prior to Vatican II, the famed theologian Ernst Troeltsch found himself accosted by similarly far-reaching questions for which no ready answer could be discerned. If the Christian tradition is to remain relevant to people's lives, he averred at the conclusion of his monumental two-volume *The Social Teaching of the Christian Churches*, "thoughts will be necessary which have not yet been thought, and which will correspond to this new situation as the older forms met the need of the social situation of earlier ages."[20] Such thoughts, in my assessment, have yet to arrive on the scene. Perhaps they never will. Undoubtedly, though, the broadly felt need for new moorings for belief and identity among American Catholics is a defining characteristic of the present situation, just as it is yet another legacy of Vatican II.

---

20. Ernst Troeltsch, *The Social Teachings of the Christian Churches* (1912; reprint, Louisville, KY: Westminster/John Knox Press, 1992), 1012.

RECASTING CONCILIAR ACHIEVEMENTS

4

Vatican Council II
Collegiality and Structures of Communion

JOHN R. QUINN

When John XXIII announced an ecumenical council, the whole world was astonished. The Roman cardinals were even more astonished. It seemed like an impulsive act lacking plan or forethought. But this was not the case. Some years before, on a visit to Padua, Cardinal Roncalli, the future John XXIII, had mentioned to the archbishop that he thought there should be a Council in the foreseeable future. As a papal nuncio during the 1940s, he was likely aware that Pope Pius XII gave some thought over a period of a year and a half to calling a Council, but then dropped the idea as premature. Another indication that he would likely have had some thoughts about a council is the fact that he was friends with some of the important theological leaders of the period such as Lambert Beauduin, and he had read the work of the French Dominican scholar Yves Congar entitled *True and False Reform in the Church*. In addition, Roncalli himself had a lifelong interest in history, had taught history in his local seminary, and he wrote a biography of one of the distinguished bishops who led the implementation of the Council of Trent, St. Charles Borromeo. All in all, then, a council was not a sudden impulse or a completely new idea for the newly elected Pope John XXIII.

Vatican Council II brought with it a whole new vocabulary to the Catholic world. One word that was destined to give rise to spirited controversy was the word *collegiality*. The idea of collegiality figured prominently in the Council document on the church, *Lumen gentium*. That document was significant also because it placed the people of

God first before treating of the pope and the bishops, and it placed the Blessed Virgin Mary in the context of the church as the first disciple in addition to her role as Mother of the Lord. Fathers of the Church with wide and enduring influence such as Augustine and Pope Leo I had also presented Our Lady as the first among the disciples.

During the period after the French Revolution, the prevailing and almost exclusive concept of the church was that it was a perfect society, a visible structure with laws and sanctions and with a structured governing authority. The reason why theologians of this period insisted that the church is a *perfect* society was to counteract some Catholic rulers who claimed that the church could not achieve its purpose without the support of the state, as though the church were a department of the state. While Vatican II (*Lumen gentium* 8) also affirms that the church is a visible society with laws, it goes more deeply and develops the ancient and biblical vision of the church as a communion.

There is no evidence in the New Testament that the church began as isolated, independent communities that later federated into a single church. From the very outset there was deeply embedded in the many communities the conviction that they were one church because they all embraced the teaching and the witness of the Twelve; they had one baptism, one faith, and one Lord; and they were all sealed with the Holy Spirit who glorifies Jesus. Vatican Council II recovered this biblical and apostolic vision of the church and made communion the foundation of everything else it taught about the church. The doctrine of collegiality is rooted in the church as communion. As we know, there has been some disagreement about collegiality. At the council, objectors claimed that any idea of collegiality between the bishops and the pope would destroy papal authority and make the pope just one more bishop. Cardinal Browne, a member of the Holy Office, said that collegiality was against the teaching of Vatican Council I on the primacy and infallibility of the pope. A fair number of objectors were canon lawyers, and they got their idea of *college* from classical Roman law. For Roman law a *college* was a body of equals all having equal authority. These objectors had little grasp of the history of the church and particularly of the synodal structures of antiquity.

The majority of the bishops at the Council, however, took another tack. This group had been influenced by a study of history and the developments of theological and biblical scholarship. Some of these theological and biblical factors will be discussed here and then some historical factors.

The nineteenth- and twentieth-century movement known as the *New Theology* (*Théologie nouvelle*) was actually not so new. It was really a recovery of the enduring sources of theology, the Bible, the early ecumenical councils and the writings of the Fathers of the Church. These fountains of Catholic doctrine showed that all the bishops of the church were as a body the heirs of the original apostles. The college of bishops is the successor of the college of the apostles. This truth was opposed by Cardinal Ottaviani, Prefect of the Holy Office, on the grounds that there was nothing in the New Testament to show that the apostles formed a college. Ottaviani and those who shared this view feared that any idea of collegiality would be injurious to the supreme and sovereign role of the pope.

But Vatican II reaffirmed the long-held teaching that priests are made bishops by the sacrament of episcopal ordination, that the episcopal office is not simply a function or an administrative role. The pope is a bishop, and so true is this that canon law states explicitly that if a priest is elected pope he is not yet in fact pope until he is ordained a bishop. So clearly the college of bishops is made up of those who have received the Holy Spirit in sacramental ordination. The first foundation of collegiality is doctrinal: the bishops and the pope are one college rooted in the sacrament of episcopal ordination.

History, the Fathers, and the ecumenical councils show that bishops had this collegial awareness from the very beginning. Even before the Emperor Constantine or the Council of Nicaea in 325, bishops had long had the practice of meeting regionally to settle disciplinary, doctrinal, and liturgical issues so that there would be order and harmony among the churches in the region. Very early these regional councils appeared, and they were collegial structures. These structures also put a brake on individual bishops striking out on their own. No bishop was a law unto himself. Every bishop was a member of the communion of the bishops. Collegiality in the church, then, is based on the truth that the church is a communion and that the bishops are a college made by sharing episcopal ordination. Collegiality is also based on the historical fact that collegial structures have been the normal way of church government from the most ancient times.

Collegiality was not invented by the Second Vatican Council. Given the antiquity of collegial structures of government in the church and its profound doctrinal foundations, it should be clear that a movement toward collegiality is not a push to transform the church into a modern democratic state. Collegial structures are operative in the first and second centuries. They were operative before Diocletian reorganized the Roman Empire late in the third century. The modern democratic state is hardly three hundred years old.

If all bishops, including the pope, are equal because they all share one and the same sacramental ordination, where do we stand in regard to the earlier objection made by some canon lawyers under the influence of classical Roman law that collegiality amounts to a rejection of papal authority? Although the bishops were all equal as sharing in one and the same sacramental ordination, from the earliest times of the ancient regional councils, there was, nevertheless, a leader among them. He was called by the Greek title *protos*. Later he was called the *archbishop*; and when larger regions were formed, the leader was called the *patriarch*. So while they were all bishops, one among them held the first place. A collection of canons dating from the fourth century states that the regional bishops "should recognize the one among them who is first and acknowledge him as head, and should do nothing extraordinary without his consent. . . . Yet neither should the one who is first do anything without the consent of all for thus there will be oneness of mind, and God will be glorified through Christ in the Holy Spirit."

The bishop of Rome held a unique place among all the bishops for several reasons. The church at Rome was the only church in which two of the chief apostles, Peter and Paul, gave the supreme witness to Christ by their martyrdom. And so modern Scripture scholars speak of the *Petrine trajectory*. By this expression they mean that in the books of the New Testament, Peter is a unique figure. His name always appears first when the lists of the Twelve are given. He is singled out by Christ and given a new name. Peter and Christ pay the Roman tax together; Paul says that the risen Lord appeared first to Peter; and while the Twelve are said to be fishers and to have the keys, only Peter is joined with Christ and commissioned to be the shepherd, as we read at the end of John's Gospel. No other member of the Twelve is commissioned as a shepherd. Throughout the New Testament, Peter is an eminent and unique figure. Scholars then refer to the Petrine trajectory as a line of development that begins with the New Testament and moves on into the history of the church. And so we see a gradual development down the centuries of the importance and the role of the bishop of Rome, who increasingly bases his central role as minister of unity and communion on his succession to the Apostle Peter. Cardinal Newman wrote that as an Anglican he came to see that there was a development in the understanding of the fundamental dogmas of faith, the Incarnation, and the Trinity, for example, and that it was thus reasonable to expect that there would also be development and growth in the church's understanding of the office of Peter in the church. In other words, the papal office in the church has undergone development and has taken different forms in different periods of history.

Both the doctrine and the long history of the church support a more collegial form of government in the church. In his homily on the Solemnity of Ss. Peter and Paul, on June 29, 2013, Pope Francis said, "Synodality is the path of the Catholic Church." Before him, Pope John Paul II declared that the collegial structures of the first millennium—synods and patriarchates—offer a way for the Catholic Church to fulfill its mission more effectively in the third millennium.

How could this be done today in a practical way? True collegiality necessarily means decentralization—that is, sharing of the governing and teaching offices in the church with the bishops rather than having all decisions and teaching come only from the pope and his Curia. A much-talked-about example comes to mind. If collegiality had been operative, the episcopal conference in the United States would have prepared and voted on its own English version of the Sacramentary. Because I can easily be misunderstood, I want to say clearly that decentralization does not mean that the bishop of Rome would cease to be the center of communion for all the local churches. But it does mean that Rome would not govern the minute details of church life everywhere in the world. I give the example of translations. But there is also the more weighty issue of the appointment of bishops, which cries out for much more meaningful participation by the bishops as well as by the clergy, religious, and laypeople of the local churches.

Some measure of decentralization would mean that collegial structures such as episcopal conferences would have much greater authority. The Second Vatican Council made the point that there is a true likeness between the ancient patriarchates and the modern episcopal conference. The patriarchates, whose origins go back to the period of the Council of Nicaea, continue in the Eastern Catholic churches today. The patriarchates still have responsibility for the appointment of bishops, the creation of dioceses, for the liturgy and its regulation, and for other substantive matters including the election of the patriarch himself. These modern Eastern Catholic patriarchates are a living example of collegiality. One practical way of true collegiality, then, would be strengthening episcopal conferences along the lines of the Eastern Catholic patriarchal structures.

It is obvious that at the present time episcopal conferences and the local churches are not ready to undertake these responsibilities. There is need to take time to work out the details of how any such structures would work in practice. Any part of a preparation for such serious responsibilities should be an examination of how these processes actually work in the Eastern Catholic churches, in the Orthodox churches and in churches of the Reformation such as the Anglican Communion. This examination would reveal the strengths and the pitfalls of such procedures. But there is also need of a substantial spiritual preparation so that bishops and their churches would understand how collegial structures in the church must be an earthly icon of the unity of the Father, the Son, and the Holy Spirit in the divine mystery of the Holy Trinity. Such an appropriation of collegial structures is not for the church simply a reorganization. It is an embrace of the great and fundamental mysteries of faith.

Another form of collegiality, the papal synod, was proposed at Vatican II. This idea gained very wide and enthusiastic support from the bishops of the world. But when it was finally enacted it was not what the bishops had hoped for. The bishops had in mind synods in which they together with the pope would share in a meaningful way in the government of the universal church. But the pope and members of the Curia were afraid that this would be injurious to the supreme authority of the pope and, as a result, the synods were limited to giving advice to the pope, which he was free to accept or reject. Nevertheless, the papal document creating the synods did make provision for a truly decision-making synod if the pope chose to do that. So the door is open and a truly decision-making synod would be possible if the pope gives it that kind of authority.

This kind of authoritative decision-making synod would not be something altogether new, dreamed up at Vatican II. Papal synods of this kind were held almost until the time of the Reformation. One of the strongest popes of the second millennium, Gregory VII, held such synods regularly, and obviously did not think they were injurious to papal authority that he was vigorous in asserting. In this context it is important to recall that Pope John Paul himself pointed explicitly to the collegial structures of the first millennium as a way for the church in the third millennium (*Ut unum sint* 55-56).

Through the whole first millennium the popes wrote no encyclicals nor did they define any dogmas of faith. The popes of the first millennium did not exercise a universal government of the whole church. The popes in their capacity as bishop of Rome and successor of Peter were the bond of communion for all the other local churches and a final court of appeal in major disputes. But they did not exercise the kind of centralized government of the whole church to which we have become accustomed. While the popes of the first millennium did exercise certain administrative functions in Europe, they did not do so in the East where they confined the papal role to maintaining the whole church in unity in faith. Thus, Joseph Ratzinger is among the well-known theologians who correctly makes the distinction between the Petrine role and the patriarchal role of the pope.[1] In simple terms, the Petrine role is the role of minister of unity and communion in the whole church. The patriarchal role is a role of unity and communion in a given region, but it involves administrative functions such as creating boundaries for a diocese, naming bishops, regulating the liturgy, and other such functions. Ratzinger says that the confusion between the pope's patriarchal role and the strictly papal role is a cause of many problems in the church, and this amalgamation of roles has led to what Ratzinger called "excessive Roman centralization."

---

1. Joseph A. Ratzinger, "Primacy and Episcopacy," *Theology Digest* 19.3 (Autumn 1971): 206.

The failure to understand the church as communion is a significant reason for opposition to collegial sharing by the pope and the bishops in teaching and government. This leads to the understanding of the papacy as a sovereignty—and sovereignty commonly means that authority is supreme, absolute, and cannot be shared. This is not the traditional theology of the church, and it is not the teaching of Vatican I or Vatican II. Even Vatican Council I, which defined the primacy of the pope, did not define that primacy in terms of sovereignty. Vatican I explicitly placed the pope within the college of bishops and was clear to affirm that the church is not a single diocese with one bishop, the pope. It said:

> The power of the supreme pontiff by no means detracts from the ordinary and immediate power of episcopal jurisdiction, by which bishops, who have succeeded to the place of the apostles by appointment of the Holy Spirit, tend and govern individually the particular flocks. . . . On the contrary, this power of theirs is asserted, supported and defended by the supreme and universal pastor. . . . (*Pastor aeternus*, c. 3)

If the pope is not an absolute sovereign, he nevertheless does have true authority, and no other single bishop has the ministry of communion and unity in the universal church. Pope John Paul states quite forthrightly that the papal ministry of unity and communion is an illusion if it does not have true authority. So to say that the pope is not an absolute sovereign does not mean that he has no true and binding authority. But in the long history of the church and in Catholic theology, the pope exercises his authority in communion. Cardinal Newman emphasized this aspect of papal authority at the time of Vatican I when he wrote about papal infallibility. He was insistent that in the history of the church prior to 1854—the year of the definition of the Immaculate Conception—all papal dogmatic definitions had been made in the context of a council, not separately by the pope. Newman did not deny that the pope in some special circumstance had authority to make definitive and binding teaching, and he used the eighteenth-century condemnation of Jansenism by Pius VI as an example of this. In holding that the condemnation of Jansenism was an infallible act of the pope, Newman was in the mainstream of theological thought at the time. But he did maintain that the normal way of exercising this kind of authority was in the context of communion with the other bishops in a council.[2]

Vatican I correctly read, like Vatican II, is no obstacle to a collegial exercise of papal authority, teaching authority, or governing authority. A collegial exercise of papal authority would broaden the input into the processes of decision making, and that input would come from wide and diverse sources, from bishops and laypeople from different parts of the world.

While the term collegiality in its proper sense refers to the pope and the bishops, there is certainly a strong call for greater participation of laypersons in the decision-making processes of the church. Pope John Paul emphasized this in speaking to the bishops of Pennsylvania and New Jersey (September 11, 2004). He told them that "ecclesial communion also 'presupposes the participation of every category of the faithful. . . .' Within a sound ecclesiology of communion, a commitment to creating better structures of participation, consultation and shared responsibility should not be misunderstood as a concession to a secular 'democratic' model of governance, but as an intrinsic requirement of the exercise of episcopal authority and a necessary means of strengthening that authority." One of Cardinal Newman's notable works was entitled *On Consulting the Faithful in Matters of Doctrine*. The title itself is an indication that Newman envisioned the participation of laypersons even in the case of doctrinal decisions by the church.

Movement in the direction of greater meaningful sharing by bishops with the pope and toward greater participation by priests, religious, and laypersons in decision making and even in doctrinal questions is definitely not a trendy capitulation to the democratic spirit of the times. Rather, it is an acknowledgment of the long and very ancient practice of the church and a witness to the profound doctrinal truth of communion in one Lord, one faith, and one baptism.

---

2. *Apologia pro vita sua* (New York: Sheed & Ward, 1946), 171.

A final word. Pope Francis in his challenging document *The Joy of the Gospel* sums up much of these ideas. He says this: "Since I am called to put into practice what I ask of others, I too must think about a conversion of the papacy ... the papacy and the central structures of the universal Church also need to hear the call to pastoral conversion. ... Excessive centralization, rather than proving helpful, complicates the Church's life and her missionary outreach" (32).

5

Unexpected, Obvious, Uncertain, Hopeful
Dei verbum and What Lies Beyond

BARBARA GREEN, O.P.

The title of this chapter, expanded, would read: Though unexpected, the Second Vatican Council happened, appearing briefly or superficially to have been obvious as its documents took promising shape. But its fruit has seemed to languish, though possibilities for a good harvest remain. What can revitalize the potential of *Dei verbum*, the Dogmatic Constitution on Divine Revelation? The plan here is to sketch first the unlikelihood that attended the challenge of moving biblical interpretation into the modern period, talk briefly about what seemed to fall eventually, if not readily, into place, and sample all too briefly some of its impact on biblical scholarship. Finally, some of the ambiguity of the document and the existential challenges of the ensuing fifty years will be considered in order to suggest what obstacles remain and how they might be managed so that the breakthrough achieved at the Council continues to produce fruit for the church and for all of good will who rely on its Scriptures.

One way to envision the issues under consideration here is to think of the Council as a doorway, majestic and grand, glimpsed from a distance. As the Roman Catholic Church moved forward in time from its origins through late antiquity into the medieval and early modern periods, the doorway creaking open in 1962 looked distant, unapproachable, and unlikely of attainment. Yet, thanks to action undertaken below the radar, some participants actually did arrive; and as they swept through the grand portals, whether congratulating themselves or murmuring trepidations—likely both—many of them, even most, turned and faced outward again or sat down soon, suggesting by analogy that a good deal of the achievement was simply their arriving at the Council. The Council as it actually happened was in many ways more about the past than about the future, a point skillfully suggested by Stephen Schloesser's setting of the 1962-65 event in its historical and social contexts (see chap. 1). Without criticizing the impulse to reverse trajectory on entering or to pause for rest rather than continue to push forward, we may venture that in the fifty years since the end of the Council and the approval of *Dei verbum*, its achievements notwithstanding, some fresh bold choices must be made if the hope of the document is to mature and bear fruit in the decades ahead.

Unexpected

What is the basis for the claim that the context needed for a revitalization of the reading of Scripture was unlikely? Consider five points. First, taking the long backward view: the Roman Catholic response to Bible-related challenges of the Western Renaissance, Reformation, and Enlightenment was basically defensive, even hostile. Openness to critical methods, to original languages (Hebrew and Greek), to diversity of viewing angle and especially to issues of authority characterizing the set of cultural earthquakes rumbling from the sixteenth through nineteenth centuries was minimal at best.[1] Second, as the nineteenth century closed, the encyclical of Leo XIII, *Providentissimus Deus* (1893), encouraged certain moves by those interpreting Scripture (e.g., acquiring skill in the "Oriental languages" of biblical composition) but implicitly or directly discouraged others (general reading of the Bible by laity, utilization of new historical methods of inquiry by scholars).[2] Yet, third, even if inexplicably and unexpectedly, some

---

1. John R. Donahue, "Bible in Roman Catholicism since *Divino Afflante Spiritu*," *Word & World* 13.4 (1993): 404-13, is one of many places the history can be reviewed. See also Joseph A. Fitzmyer, "Scripture in the Catholic Tradition," in *Living Traditions of the Bible: Scripture in Jewish, Christian, and Muslim Practice*, ed. James G. Bowley (St. Louis, MO: Chalice Press, 1999), 145-61.

2. John W. O'Malley, *What Happened at Vatican II* (Cambridge, MA: Harvard University Press, 2010), 68.

"Bible study" seeds were planted among laity and scholars and took root, though remaining fragile and endangered. A fourth disincentive to reform emerged in 1907 in the massive condemnation of a set of views called Modernism, rendering all but impossible the nurturing of those seeds, as scholars were placed under severe threat of punishment.[3] But, fifth, in 1943, Pius XII's encyclical *Divino afflante Spiritu* provided fresh and unexpected encouragement for those persevering in fresh approaches to the study of the Bible, for example, encouraging newer critical methods and minimizing older figural ones, nurturing the small plants that were about to bear amazing fruit.[4]

So the document emerging in 1965 was surely unlikely and unexpected, with the uncertainty of leadership and the vacillation of official stances weighing against it, since the study necessary for modern interpretation of ancient classics requires years of patience, skill, discipline, and insight. The tortuous path to *Divino afflante Spiritu*, with its hills and valleys and switchbacks, gave substantial hint that there would be resistance at the Council doorway and just beyond—as there was, stretching even to our own time of celebration fifty years later.

Obvious

Once the Council doors had been entered and the work of drafting documents begun, progress on the document on Divine Revelation was relentless and inexorable, even fast by ordinary measures of ecclesial progress. The process of the drafts that would emerge as *Dei verbum* is documented at length elsewhere.[5] Here are a few points on the substantial achievement of *Dei verbum* and some fault lines in the document.

Dei verbum consists of a preface and six chapters. The preface, in continuity with past teaching and conciliar proclamation, claims the document to be the authentic teaching about revelation and the

---

3. Donahue, "Bible in Roman Catholicism," 406; O'Malley, *What Happened at Vatican II*, 68-70.

4. Donahue, "Bible in Roman Catholicism," 407; O'Malley, *What Happened at Vatican II*, 84.

5. Ronald D. Witherup, *Scripture: Dei verbum* (Mahwah, NJ: Paulist Press, 2006). O'Malley's study of the Council devotes many pages to this point as well.

process of its transmission, making clear the gift of salvation to the world, envisioning it as an invitation to fellowship with a relational God. The first chapter talks in more detail about God's self-disclosure through Jesus Christ and in the Holy Spirit, with divine purposes made visible in history and proclaimed and clarified in Scripture. This divine gift, rising from creation and from God's dealings with the Hebrew/Jewish people, comes together in Christ, mediator and fullness of revelation, establishing an eternal covenant never to pass away. The document indicates that no further public revelation is awaited. The response to God's initiative is faith-filled and free obedience to God's gifts, made accessible to reason through revelation.

The second chapter, making use of both the dynamics of ongoing appropriation and the more static imagery of "deposit," talks about the transmission of revelation, beginning with the Hebrew prophets and culminating in the Gospels. Scripture is a mirror through which the church contemplates God. What is handed on is what is needed for the life and holiness of the church, content that develops in the tradition of the church. God continuously converses with the church, and through the church the voice of Scripture resounds. Both Scripture and tradition flow from the divine wellspring of truth, together constituting revelation, both entrusted to the teaching office of the church. The church is not above the Word of God but serves it.

A third chapter maintains that all books of the Old and New Testaments are sacred and canonical, having God as their author, containing all that God intended to be made available in sacred writings for the sake of salvation, with the complex and fraught claims of inspiration, infallibility, and inerrancy named but skated over. Interpreters of Scripture are bidden, freshly, to investigate the intent of the human author as well as the divine, to take careful note of literary forms used while maintaining as well the content and unity of Scripture and tradition. Scripture, true and holy, is still envisioned as a remarkable condescension of eternal wisdom into human language, recalling the incarnation of God's eternal word into human flesh and weakness.

A fourth chapter asserts the permanent value of the Old Testament, with the New Testament hidden in the Old, the Old Testament made manifest in the New. That is, the two testaments are in dialogical relationship. The New Testament, the focus of chapter 5, again refers to the Incarnation of the Word in flesh, bearing witness to the realities of Christ's words, deeds, death, resurrection, ascension, and sending of the Holy Spirit. The Gospels have preeminence in this witness to the life and teaching of the incarnate Word, historically and faithfully transmitting what Jesus Christ did and taught for salvation, composed from events of his life, from the developing tradition, taking shape in the written documents. There is no claim that all the material has been included within the biblical books.

Finally, a sixth chapter makes some additional claims about Sacred Scripture in the life of the church, liturgical, sacramental, theological: The church venerates Scripture as it does the body of the Lord, receiving and offering from both the bread of life. Easy access to Scripture should be provided by good and reliable vernacular versions, granting that the Greek (Septuagint) and Latin (Vulgate) hold pride of place among translations. Exegetes and scholars of Scripture are invited to study that enlightens the mind, strengthens the will, and sets human hearts on fire with love of God. Theology is to be rejuvenated by the careful scrutiny of Scripture in the light of faith. Clergy and other ministers of the word are to hold fast to Scripture through reading, study, and prayer, as are Christian faithful urged to engage Scripture in liturgy and devotional practices, including study and prayer. [6]

Council Achievements

Any inquiry into the process that eventually led to the document on Sacred Scripture, so serenely summarized above, will make clear how

---

6. For a convenient summary of ways in which *Dei verbum* demonstrates continuity with previous teaching, on the one hand, and seems to break with it, on the other, see Witherup, *Scripture*. His summary is immensely helpful. To lift out simply one continuity and one break: "Sacred Scripture is God's Word in human words; the Bible communicates faithfully and without error God's sacred message" (p. 44); and "Coupled with the theme above [God's role in the production of Scripture via revelation and inspiration] is an emphasis on the human dimension of producing the Sacred Scriptures. Not only is there explicit acknowledgment of the need to pay attention to literary forms and other influences on literary expression in the original biblical languages, but it is stated that the goal of interpretation is to uncover 'the intention of the sacred writers (*DV* 12)'" (pp. 49-50).

many potentially thorny issues were worded so as to achieve consensus.[7] Granting that multiple fault lines underlying the document were obscured, still it is clear that *Dei verbum* moves well beyond many of the positions enunciated at the Council of Trent and previously, endorsing a widespread embrace of Scripture in liturgy, in church teaching and catechesis, in academic study, and in the life of faith among believers. Before looking at some of those unstable places where significant work remains to be done—or progress stalled or reversed—I will provide examples of the sort of study enabled and encouraged by the Council and its documents.

The past fifty years have seen a remarkable harvest of achievements in biblical studies. Undeniable is the immense and fruitful impact of modern and critical methods of reading Scripture, both in scholarship and in lived experience, bearing results in academia and in worship, with the original historical methodology named by the document blossoming into literary and reader-oriented modes of reading and interpreting. The turn to language in both philosophy and literary studies has emerged most usefully in the study of hermeneutics, the consideration of how texts "mean" and how we understand as we do when we read them, ancient and sacred texts not least.[8] Contemporary hermeneutics has been fruitful in positioning both modern study and precritical or classical readings, those characteristics of both the rabbis and Christian commentators before the Western Renaissance, Reformation, and Enlightenment, so that each has clear and sensible aims and neither need scorn the accomplishments of the other. Different eras have distinct assumptions, hopes, and projects, and the two modes of interpretation (precritical and modern), often seen as adversaries, can in fact be collaborators, once we understand what each is desirous of doing and able to accomplish. *Dei verbum* and its spacious language have underwritten ecumenical and interreligious dialogue fruitfully, also welcoming the fresh contributions made by

---

7. Witherup, *Scripture*, 54-58.

8. For a thorough explanation of how hermeneutics contributes to the interpretation of the Bible and to the Bible as Scripture, consult Sandra M. Schneiders, *The Revelatory Text: Interpreting the New Testament as Sacred Scripture*, 2d ed. (Collegeville, MN: Liturgical Press, 1999).

global voices, so that the views and insights of those not previously included have been welcomed, for example, women, the poor, communities outside the Anglo-European world. A significant deepening of the appreciation of the validity and beauty of Jewish interpretation has come forth from the rather minimal praise given the Old Testament, and indeed there has been an increased awareness of the harm done by too great a rush to seeing the Old Testament's value only insofar as it seems to anticipate the coming of Jesus the Christ, or through supersessionist assumptions and interpretations. The document helped make clear the importance of moving beyond ransacking the Bible as a source of prooftexts and a compendium of timeless dogmatic truths to appreciating it as a set of texts with compelling depth of meaning and beauty of language. The Common Lectionary has expanded the scope of biblical material included in weekday and Sunday liturgy, selecting pairs of readings that highlight ways in which the Hebrew Scripture is matched or made more visible in the life of Jesus (granting that the Old Testament remains underexposed and the presumption for selecting readings still tends to be typological).

In addition to those vast and general gains, individual books of the Bible have in the last decades enjoyed fresh scrutiny, with methods and results not possible or likely before the work of the Second Vatican Council. One brief sample from each testament must suffice to indicate how scholars are now encouraged to read both with the aid of more critical tools and diverse perspectives and also with greater sensitivity toward and accuracy about the Jewish people and tradition.

In regard to the book of Jonah: Christian interpretation, over the centuries, has tended to focus on the fate of the Ninevites, sensing that the book is primarily about Gentiles rather than about Jews. And Christian commentators have assessed Jonah as somewhat flawed in his unwillingness to minister to the people of Nineveh: first refusing, then reluctant and plausibly churlish, eventually as resentful that those to whom he preached have been offered a reprieve and survive. But to take more seriously the identity of Jonah's audience is to appreciate the implications of their being Assyrians, taking their particular "Ninevite" name from the capital of that empire, itself an oppressor of the peoples of Israel and Judah from at least the eighth to the seventh century and intermittently before that. To drop into place that piece of historical information opens the eyes of Christian interpreters to the reality that Jonah was specifically charged by God to help the enemies of his own people avoid destruction. The problems facing such a prophet assume a much more complex nature, long familiar to Jewish interpreters who have explored with variety the challenges Jonah faced, providing sensible reasons for him to have wanted to avoid his assignment. Christians are invited to become less critical of his first refusal and more sympathetic to his reasons for resisting his assignment and the Gentile part in such matters.[9]

Matthew's Gospel can be appreciated freshly as well, in the wake of studies accompanied, supported, and prompted by the Council document on the interpretation of Scripture. Discovery and study of the Dead Sea Scrolls has brought a greater and more accurate engagement with Second Temple Jewish literature, helping Christians recognize the deeply Jewish nature of the Gospel. Many of the small forms within the Gospel use Jewish modes of speech seamlessly, as makes sense once the continuity with Judaism is appreciated. Samples include the form of the beatitudes (the "blessed are you" sayings),[10] the *pesher*-like mode of interpretation (the interpretation of past prophecy to apply to present circumstances),[11] the stipulation of criteria for judgment that one finds in apocalyptic judgment scenes (Matthew 5:3-11 and 25:31-46) and the penal codes of the Dead Sea sect (the Rule of the Community and the Damascus Document).[12]

---

9. For more information on any of these points, consult Barbara Green, *Jonah's Journeys* (Collegeville, MN: Liturgical Press, 2005).

10. I am indebted to my colleague Catherine M. Murphy specifically for this information on the New Testament and for general fruitful collaboration as well. See Joseph A. Fitzmyer, "A Palestinian Collection of Beatitudes," in *The Four Gospels 1992: Festschrift Frans Neirynck*, ed. Frans van Segbroeck and Christopher M. Tuckett; 2 vols., Bibliotheca ephemeridum theologicarum, lovaniensium 100 (Louvain: Peeters, 1992), 1:509-15; Benedict Viviano, "Eight Beatitudes at Qumran and in Matthew? A New Publication from Cave Four," *Svensk Exegetisk Årsbok* 58 (1993) 71-84.

11. Maurya P. Horgan, *Pesharim: Qumran Interpretations of Biblical Books*, Catholic Biblical Quarterly Monograph Series 8 (Washington, DC: Catholic Biblical Association, 1979).

12. For general background, see John J. Collins, "Wisdom, Apocalypticism,

The Gospel's presentation of Pharisees and the assignment of blood guilt to the crowd calling for Jesus' crucifixion (Matthew 27:25) can be recognized as anachronistic and tendentious, articulated to demonstrate the advantage of what Jesus is offering his peers over against the diverse viewpoints current in Judaism at the time the Gospel reached final form at the end of the first century.[13]

Council Compromises and Present Crossroads

But the strength of *Dei verbum* duly acknowledged and celebrated, the question is how to move forward beyond the potential claimed fifty years ago and the various challenges emerging since then. There is no doubt plenty of room for more of the same fruit that has just been sampled, but where is the next genuine movement to come from, assuming that another Council is not imminent?

It is clear in retrospect—even at the time for those watching carefully—that certain key issues needing inclusion in the document were not ready for thorough discussion at the Council. In order to gain the sort of endorsement desired for this document (others as well), language that would bridge and not offend was sought, and general statements were offered and approved at face value rather than their implications being worked through.[14] To some extent that choice was inevitable, since the nuances of complex topics are not well suited for assembly negotiation, especially where multiple languages and levels

---

and Generic Compatibility," in *In Search of Wisdom: Essays in Memory of John G. Gammie*, ed. Leo G. Perdue, Bernard Brandon Scott, and William Johnston Wiseman (Louisville, KY: Westminster/John Knox, 1993), 165-85.

13. Daniel J. Harrington, "The Gradual Emergence of the Church and the Parting of the Ways," in *Christ Jesus and the Jewish People Today*, ed. Philip A. Cunningham, Joseph Sievers, Mary Boys, and Hans Hermann Hendrix (Grand Rapids, MI: William B. Eerdmans, 2011), 92-104. See also the Pontifical Biblical Commission, "The Jewish People and Their Sacred Scriptures in the Christian Bible" (Vatican City: Vatican Press, 2002); Roland E. Murphy, "The Biblical Commission, The Jews, and Scriptures," *Biblical Theology Bulletin* 32.3 (2002): 145-49; and Amy-Jill Levine, "Roland Murphy, the Pontifical Commission, Jews, and the Bible," *Biblical Theology Bulletin* 33.3 (2003): 104-13.

14. See Witherup, *Scripture*, 29, for a chart and his whole Part I for a discussion.

of competence are involved. Nor were certain of the embedded issues ripe for exploration by those assembled. So let me now offer some views on places where the Council fathers papered over rather than explored serious fault lines, these rifts having become only clearer in the past fifty years. Four points will suffice to suggest an agenda for future progress in biblical interpretation without implying that they are the only issues at hand.

First, though the document makes a breakthrough by resisting the long-standing and polarized topic of whether there is one source of revelation or two, *Dei verbum* suggests that the one divine wellspring of revelation generates both Scripture and tradition. Unresolved, however, is the issue of what and what kind of authority Scripture exercises in relation to both the faithful and over the magisterium. How best can the Pontifical Biblical Commission proceed as it learns and teaches about Scripture and collaborates with others who do so as well?[15]

Second, the document toggles somewhat between presenting Scripture in propositionalist and personalist terms. The more classic propositional model emphasizes static truths to be assented to, while the personalist stresses the offer of relationship, presupposing engagement and exploration. In the propositionalist model, it is clear that revelation is complete, but that claim makes less sense in the personalist way of thinking, where the challenge to those engaged with Scripture (both personally and professionally) is to deepen constantly the capacity for understanding. How to correlate these clashing frameworks appropriately, perhaps to affirm one as more helpful than the other?

Third, the document maintains an ambiguous stance toward historical and "scientific" approaches to both Scripture and tradition. Though the long-standing and powerful resistance toward newer

---

15. An address of John Paul II to the Pontifical Biblical Commission (Béchard, *Scripture Documents*, 167ff.) highlights the issue. Addressing the issue of the interpretation of the Bible in the church directly (p. 169, paragraph 4), he notes that the Council document approved the "scientific study of 'literary genres'" while also warning against "an abuse of historical analysis, called 'diachronic,' an analysis exclusively 'synchronic,' devoid of any historical dimension." He calls for inclusion of the Holy Spirit within the process of interpretation, also of theology. But how so?

methods of inquiry (modern methods) is absent from *Dei verbum* and subsequent documents, with provision made for investigating the human choices and cultural contexts presiding over the biblical writings, resistance to modern methods has waxed rather than waned in the past decades. There is need for a consistent welcome to newer methods and the demonstration that they can be fruitful for study and for the spiritual life (as classically conceived, since of course study is also spiritual).

Fourth, though mentioning the two terms "inspiration" and "inerrancy," the document says relatively little to clarify how the meanings of these words and their fresh understanding may be approached. Inspiration, and the resulting inerrancy, is claimed not to be verbal but something broader: The Bible teaches without error on matters "which God wanted put into sacred writings for the sake of salvation" (*Dei verbum*, 11). Insofar as God is the author of Scripture, error is not an issue. But the claim of the document remains general, and so the particulars actually embedded in the question are not probed. What model of inspiration is to be assumed, and though it is difficult to explain, how does it operate? What "things" does God consider important for salvation and what other matters, presumably not vital, are not "covered" by God's seal? In a diverse church community where fundamentalism is present (within and outside the walls), how might inspiration be better described so as to avoid some of the problems that have dogged the notion?

Anticipated

In all of these instances, if the document is to "grow into its own potential" usefully, discussion needs to progress on clarifying the implications and growing edge of *Dei verbum*. Since space precludes an adequate discussion of the past fifty years' worth of commentary on this Council document, let us offer three more general points of interest and concern. First is the matter of change and the degree to which historical change is officially acknowledged as operative in church matters. John O'Malley, treating this as one of three central issues that was unresolved during the Council (and I suspect he would also say since), reviews the significance of the dispute about whether growth and development of cultural reality in all its dimensions can be acknowledged and exploited or whether it remains necessary to affirm a sort of ahistorical platonic sense of things, where realities remain much as they always have appeared to be—with genuine historical investigations also disqualified.[16] Insofar as the need for and benefit of change are denied, and insofar as classic ways of understanding remain supreme, little genuine progress will be made on how Scripture is to be read, understood, interpreted, with the antique and medieval periods allowed to be different from the modern and it from them. This, of course, is also an authority issue, since those who deny the reality of change are prone to deny that there is much need for reform. The alternative is to welcome conversation about multiplicity in a complex living and multicultural community like the Catholic Church, such that the needed stress on continuity can be balanced by discussion of how, specifically, theory and practice have developed over years and will continue to do so. Absent this perspective, there will be little give on discussion of biblical interpretation.

A second point concerns the relationship between the magisterium and Scripture, specifically between the church's official teachers and the larger and more heterodox scholarly body of professional biblical interpreters. That the bishops are the official teachers is not disputed, but continuously problematic is the question of how their authority is appropriately exercised. The Pontifical Biblical Commission (PBC), existing as part of that teaching office, has issued documents from the end of the Council going forward, and the news is promising on the one hand but much less so on the other.[17] The main and summative discussion of biblical interpretation (issued in 1993), "On

---

16. O'Malley, *What Happened at Vatican II*, 290-313.

17. The Pontifical Biblical Commission, appointed just at the start of the twentieth century and then reconstituted after the Council, functioning as part of the Congregation for the Doctrine of the Faith and comprising a small number of (primarily Anglo-European) churchmen, continues the conversation about issues raised in *Dei verbum*. See Dean P. Béchard, ed. and trans., *The Scripture Documents: An Anthology of Official Catholic Teachings* (Collegeville, MN: Liturgical Press, 2002). Popes John Paul II and Benedict XVI have written revealingly on the state of affairs.

the Interpretation of the Bible in the Church,"[18] has been generally recognized as a balanced and helpful presentation of the range of critical methods currently in use by Catholic (and of course other) scholars, carefully affirming responsible use of such methods.[19] However, as is the case with most documents that remain at a fairly general level, the more urgent issue is how the documents are actually interpreted and implemented, particularly by the authorities themselves. The issuance of *Verbum Domini*, a postsynodal apostolic exhortation issued by Benedict XVI in 2010,[20] is held by some to be a backtracking by the pontiff on both the 1993 PBC document and on *Dei verbum* itself; others see continuity. The sense of a small circle of classically trained Anglo-European men as adequate to manage this huge topic seems most outdated, especially in an era where Catholic biblical scholarship has come of age and many voices once excluded are contributing usefully.

More ominous are examples of how interpretation actually works by those closest to official circles in the Catholic Church. Two examples will suggest this more troubling trajectory. In 1976 the PBC, asked to opine on the biblical contribution to the troublesome question of the ordination of women in the Roman Catholic Church, reported that there was insufficient data available for a definitive answer.[21] Before its work was officially reported, the commission was disbanded, though its views eventually emerged. In the meantime, official pronouncements on the position of women have proceeded without the sort of careful and critical work on biblical texts that the documents seem to endorse. Ideology seems to trump exegesis. Similarly, the published

---

18. Béchard, *Scripture Documents*, 244-317.

19. For particulars, see the set of three reviews of the document, commissioned by First Things (August-September 1994); http://www.firstthings.com/article/2007/10/interpretingthebiblethreeviews38 (accessed August 12, 2013).

20. The document may be found at http://www.fmverbumdei.com/familia/index.php/en/verbumdomini (accessed August 18, 2013).

21. For a thorough discussion of this matter, consult Deborah Halter, *The Papal No: A Comprehensive Guide to the Vatican's Rejection of Women's Ordination* (New York: Crossroad, 2004).

work of Benedict XVI on Jesus,[22] notably his work on the infancy narratives, evinces little ongoing engagement with the critical issues raised about that complex biblical material in the decades since the Council. That the author, himself so heavily involved with the PBC documents, seems to disregard the very principles developing from *Dei verbum* on through the PBC document of 1993, is disconcerting to say the very least. The issues raised so boldly at the Council are cast into doubt by the refusal of the author of this book on an admittedly challenging set of texts to make use of critical methods.

Third, and related—as all these issues are—is the question of responsible hermeneutics. How does language really mean, even when the text in question is ancient and canonical, as of course the Bible is? How, specifically, can tradition continue to be shown relevant more than two thousand years past its production? How can a bold and competent exposition of hermeneutical theory establish both the value of the past understandings of biblical texts while also allowing fresh insights to emerge, thanks to new insights and understandings? It is disconcerting and demoralizing when positions are taught with the claim of biblical warrant or when the most authoritative voices in the church—whether writing as pope or as private citizen (or both)—appear to ignore, disregard, or event flout the most fundamental tenets of critical methodology when writing on biblical matters.

The pontificate of Francis seems hopeful. *Dei verbum* is a wonderful document, saying a lot and implying more. If it is to come into its own and continue to show the promise indicated fifty years ago, these three basic matters as well as others alluded to above need frank and extended discussion, a possibility that seems more likely than before. Perhaps the time is at hand.

---

22. Joseph Ratzinger, *Jesus of Nazareth: The Infancy Narratives*, trans. Philip J. Whitmore (London: Burns & Oates, 2012).

6

Gaudium et spes *and the Call to Justice* The U.S. Experience

KRISTIN HEYER AND BRYAN MASSINGALE

As John O'Malley aptly puts it, the spirit of Vatican II was marked by "friendship, partnership, kinship, reciprocity, dialogue, collegiality"—a different way of being church. It is fair to say that *Gaudium et spes* (GS), the Council's Pastoral Constitution on the Church in the Modern World, exemplifies these broader shifts. Its tone, substance, and posture reflect this move from "commands to invitations, from laws to ideals, from threats to promises, from coercion to conscience, from monologue to dialogue, from ruling to serving, from exclusion to inclusion, from hostility to friendship, from fault-finding to appreciation, and from behavior-modification to inner appropriation of values."[1] The Council's articulation of its social mission in solidarity with all of humankind in this, its final and longest document, marks a dramatic departure from the church's traditionally defensive, reactionary stance toward the world. *Gaudium et spes* ushers in an open stance that takes seriously the struggles of those "in any way afflicted." In this chapter, some of the historical background and key themes of this landmark document, particularly as they have influenced social justice activism, ministry, and controversies in the United States context, are presented, raising the question of how these themes might play out in a new era for the church.

The Document's Historical Context

Among the Council's four constitutions, two focus on the church itself: *Lumen gentium* looks inward, to the renewal of the church's

---

1. John O'Malley, "The Council's Spirit: Vatican II: The Time for Reconciliation," *Conversations on Jesuit Higher Education* 42 (Fall 2012): 2-6, at 6.

self-understanding and structures, and *Gaudium et spes* addresses the relationship between church and contemporary world in all its pluralism and complexity. In the latter we encounter the Council's shift away from conceiving of church and world (or the sacred and secular realms) in opposition to each other, and toward engaging social questions as central to the church's very mission and identity. This dialogical style signaled a clear departure from the defensive siege mentality, which O'Malley has characterized as the "long nineteenth century," basic elements of which prevailed up to the evening of Vatican II. [2]

With the wealthy European elites seen to be the church's allies, the pre-Vatican II church denounced human rights, labor unions, religious toleration, and interreligious dialogue as dangerous. O'Malley notes that the Council

> did not want to change the Church into a democracy, as its repeated affirmations of papal authority demonstrate beyond question. But it did want to redefine how authority was to function, for instance, with a respect for conscience that transformed the members of the Church from "subjects" into "participants." . . . Vatican II did not want the Church to abdicate its privileged role as teacher of the Gospel, but it insisted that the Church, like all good teachers, needed to learn as it taught. [3]

The initial lines of *Gaudium et spes* signal these major changes in posture, mission, and methodology:

> The joys and hope, the grief and anguish of the people of our time, especially of those who are poor or afflicted, are the joys and hopes, the grief and anguish of the followers of Christ as well. Nothing that is genuinely human fails to find an echo in their hearts. For theirs is a community of people united in age towards the Father's kingdom, bearers of a message of salvation for all of humanity. That is why they cherish a feeling of deep solidarity with the human race and its history. [4]

---

2. John O'Malley, "The Style of Vatican II: The 'How' of the Church Changed during the Council," *America* (February 24, 2003): 12-15, at 14.

3. Ibid., 15.

4. *Gaudium et spes*, in Austin Flannery, O.P., ed., *Vatican Council II: The*

Here we find a radical shift away from the "long nineteenth century." Rather than the church saying, "We have the answers, now by the way, what are your questions?" it is starting with the actual questions facing humanity in a given time and place, particularly those afflicted or suffering. *Gaudium et spes* exemplifies the conciliar shift away from conceiving of church and world in opposition to each other, calling instead for dialogue with the world and an examination of social, cultural, and political realities in the light of the gospel. No other Vatican decree is addressed so explicitly to the wider Christian community and people outside the church, noting in paragraph 3: "The Council can provide no more eloquent proof of its solidarity with the entire human family with which it is bound up, as well as its respect and love for that family, than by engaging with it in conversation about these various problems."

The Document's Content

Thus the church's social teaching becomes bolstered with ecclesiological grounding; in other words, no longer was its social teaching considered only as a narrow category within moral theology, or something "extra," that is speaking only to the outside world, but rather it came to be chiefly conceived of as a means of fulfilling the church's very mission.[5] In *Gaudium et spes* the Council urges Christians, as "citizens of two cities," to attend to earthly duties in light of the spirit of the gospel. The document grants the ambivalent nature of worldly concerns, yet warns against total rejection of worldly activity as a substitute for discernment and selective engagement. It condemns an attitude of otherworldliness that deemphasizes earthly duties on the view that our only abiding city is that which is to come.[6] The document calls the church to political engagement to protect human dignity, without conflating the Catholic faith with particular political systems. While this indirect

---

Basic Sixteen Documents (Northport, NY: Costello Publishing Company, 1996). This source is used throughout this chapter.

5. Richard McBrien, "Catholic Social Action," *National Catholic Reporter* 14 (March 3, 1978): 7-8, as cited in Timothy G. McCarthy, *The Catholic Tradition: The Church in the Twentieth Century*, 2d ed. (Chicago: Loyola Press, 1998), 260.

6. *Gaudium et spes*, 43.

role for the church's engagement in the political order entails endless distinctions and decisions, the effort must be made precisely because the alternatives to an indirect engagement are equally unacceptable: a politicized church or a church in retreat from human affairs. The first erodes the transcendence of the gospel; the second betrays the incarnational dimension of Christian faith.

The Council's shift away from suspicion of worldly engagement rests on on its understanding the human person as the bond between the church and the world. The Council affirms the church's duty to safeguard human dignity and promote human rights, and cultivate the unity of the human family.[7] The first Council to do so, *Gaudium et spes* cites Gen 1:26-27 (humans' creation in the image and likeness of God) to develop its teaching on human dignity and rights, spelling out at length the universal rights and duties that flow from the dignity of having been created in the divine image. Whereas Pope John XXIII in his 1963 encyclical *Pacem in terris* had moved the church from "opposition to modern rights and freedoms to active engagement in the global struggle for human rights," the Council develops the church's approach to human rights further, situating its treatment of rights within the context of human interdependence.[8]

The church's public engagement should characterized by a spirit of respectful dialogue, exemplified in the opening lines of the document cited above. Pope John XXIII used the phrase "analyzing the signs of times" (in a largely empirical sense) rather than exploring abstract ideas of church and common good. This emphasis recurs throughout the Pastoral Constitution, reflecting a methodological change from a classicist to a historically conscious approach.[9] Scrutinizing the "signs of the times" and seeking to detect the meaning of emerging history, while at the same time sharing the aspirations and questionings of

---

7. *Gaudium et spes*, 40-42.

8. David Hollenbach, S.J., "Commentary on *Gaudium et spes*," in Kenneth Himes, OFM, et al., eds., *Modern Catholic Social Teaching: Commentaries and Interpretations* (Washington, DC: Georgetown University Press, 2005), 266-91, at 280-81.

9. Lois Lorentzen, "*Gaudium et spes*," in *The New Dictionary of Catholic Social Thought*, ed. Judith Dwyer (Collegeville, MN: Liturgical Press, 1994), 406-16, at 407.

all those who want to build a more human world, are the dialogical charges issued in *Gaudium et spes*. Catholic engagement with the world and its transformation by the penetration of gospel values should be marked by a spirit of dialogue and service and by what some have called a "confident modesty," mindful that the church both teaches and learns from the world.[10] It is not insignificant, then, that theologians who had been previously banned were invited to the Council; bishops and theologians were learning from each other there, exemplifying to some degree this spirit of reciprocity and humility.

By the later sessions of the Council, concern had shifted to justice throughout the world and the social questions taken up became global in scope. This marked a significant move beyond the European-dominated concerns of the pre-Vatican II church. In *Gaudium et spes*, the Council makes clear the interrelated nature of questions of international economics and peace.[11] With the proliferation of new kinds of weapons the Council recommends a fresh scrutiny of long-standing just war teachings given new threats to civilians and the harms posed by the arms race. It emphasizes the detrimental impact of persons being ruled by economics rather than vice versa, insisting that human labor is not a commodity. Its affirmation of the common purpose of all created things forms a backdrop to its teaching on private property, insisting the right to private property must yield to the cry of the poor.[12] *Gaudium et spes* insists that the obligation to help the poor is central to Christian life, not just a consideration once one's own needs are met or normal class status symbols acquired. Finally, the document presents a more personalist approach to marriage that emphasizes conjugal love, yet leaves contraception unaddressed, given that Pope Paul VI removed it from the Council's competence in 1964.

---

10. William J. Gould, "Fr. J. Bryan Hehir: Priest, Policy Analyst, and Theologian of Dialogue," in *Religious Leaders and Faith-Based Politics: Ten Profiles*, ed. Jo Renee Formicola and Hubert Morken (Lanham, MD: Rowman & Littlefield, 2001), 197-223, at 201.

11. Judith A. Merkle, SNDdeN, *From the Heart of the Church: The Catholic Social Tradition* (Collegeville, MN: Liturgical Press, 2004), 120.

12. Ibid., 121.

Impact and Reception in the U.S. Context

The dialogical engagement with wider society central to *Gaudium et spes* is evident in theological, pastoral, and social movements in subsequent decades across the globe—from liberation and feminist theologies to renewed commitments to justice on the part of Catholic educational institutions and Catholic involvement in the civil rights movement.

Catholic Presence in the Struggle for Racial Justice

One of the most immediate areas in which *Gaudium et spes* made its impact felt in the United States concerned Catholic participation in the struggle for racial justice and the civil rights movement. This movement was one of the largest and most sustained faith-based movements for social change in U.S. history.[13] Sadly, however, Catholic participation in it was woefully inadequate, almost to the point of nonexistence. A telling anecdote reveals the Catholic absence by the observation that in August 1962, it was reported that "nine Catholic laypeople" journeyed from Chicago to Albany (Georgia) to support a local effort against racial segregation. A contemporary historian observes that when contemporaries reported that this group was "the largest group of American Catholics that has participated in the nonviolent movement," it emphatically underscores "how minuscule the Catholic presence in the civil rights movement had been until that point."[14]

Among the many factors responsible for Catholic passivity and absence in the justice struggle, of particular note for this essay is the abstract character of official teaching on racial justice in the United States. To cite but one example, the 1958 statement of the U.S. bishops, "Discrimination and the Christian Conscience," issued in the aftermath of the 1954 historic Supreme Court decision outlawing

---

13. For further discussion of the civil rights movement, see Charles Marsh, *God's Long Summer: Stories of Faith and Civil Rights* (Princeton, NJ: Princeton University Press, 2008).

14. John T. McGreevy, *Parish Boundaries: The Catholic Encounter with Race in the Twentieth-Century Urban North* (Chicago: University of Chicago Press, 1996), 142.

segregation in educational institutions, forthrightly concluded that enforced segregation could not be reconciled with the Christian view of the human person. However, unlike statements issued by other national religious bodies at the time, the bishops offered no concrete guidance or recommendations for implementing this teaching. Protestant statements tended to be more concrete, calling for support of the Supreme Court decision, the integration of church facilities, support for black voting rights, and condemnation of the Ku Klux Klan. None of this specificity was found in official Catholic teaching. Catholics thus were never summoned to be proactive agents pursuing racial justice. On the contrary, despite the clear moral conclusion they reached, the bishops also betrayed a deep suspicion of what they called "rash impetuosity"—which many took as a not thinly veiled critique of the tactics used by Martin Luther King, Jr. In other words, there was never a summons for Catholics to see themselves in solidarity with the victims of injustice, and no call to actively participate in dismantling an unjust social situation.[15] As a result, the noted black Catholic historian, Cyprian Davis, concludes with characteristic understatement, "By and large Catholics, either black or white, were not in the forefront of the civil rights movement or among the leadership of the protest organizations."[16] By 1965, there was a decisive, even dramatic shift in Catholic attitudes and presence in the struggle for racial justice. Davis reports that when King gave a summons for the nation's religious leaders to come to Selma, Alabama, for a show of support for the voting rights march then underway, the response from white Catholic

---

15. For an analysis of this 1958 document, see Bryan N. Massingale, *Racial Justice and the Catholic Church* (Maryknoll, NY: Orbis Books, 2010), 50-55. For an examination of how the stance of the bishops was reflected in the guidance of leading Catholic ethicists of the time who warned against "agitation" in the quest for racial justice, see "African American Experience and U.S. Roman Catholic Ethics: 'Strangers and Aliens No Longer?'" in *Black and Catholic: The Challenge and Gift of Black Folk: Contributions of African American Experience and World View to Catholic Theology*, ed. Jamie T. Phelps (Milwaukee, WI: Marquette University Press, 1997), 79-101.

16. Cyprian Davis, *The History of Black Catholics in the United States* (New York: Crossroad, 1990), 256.

priests and sisters was "enormous."[17] Despite the opposition from the local bishop, "priests from fifty different dioceses, laypeople, and nuns flocked to Alabama," many with the support and blessing of their bishops and major superiors.[18] Newspapers and TV news reports of the time showed the then startling images of nuns in full traditional habits marching in protest marches across the country. Justifying her participation in racial justice protests, one Mother Superior declared, "It is right that we should suffer and show our suffering when—in Selma or anywhere—any of God's children are oppressed."[19]

What accounts for such a dramatic turnaround? Historians and activists of the time attribute this decisive shift to the influence of the Second Vatican Council and, more specifically, to the impact of *Gaudium et spes*. As stated earlier, Vatican II ushered in a new understanding of the church's relationship with the modern world and contemporary society. It summoned Catholics to act to improve society, not simply reject it. But more importantly, it summoned Catholics to a stance of solidarity and identification with the plight of the poor and the marginalized. Indeed, the opening words of *Gaudium et spes*, of which we can hear echoes in the words of the woman religious cited above, became the most fervent exhortation uttered by U.S. Catholic social activists throughout the 1960s. [20]

These words, and the pivotal shift they signaled, unleashed unprecedented Catholic initiatives focused on racial issues and urban poverty in the Catholic faith community. For example, in the Archdiocese of Detroit, then Cardinal Dearden convened a series of conferences in 1965 devoted to the subject of "Human Dignity" in that racially divided city. He explicitly connected this program with Vatican II and *Gaudium et spes*, as he informed the 1,500 participants that the Pastoral Constitution "begins by calling attention to the fact that we, the

---

17. Ibid., 256.

18. McGreevy, *Parish Boundaries*, 155-56.

19. Cited in McGreevy, *Parish Boundaries*, 156. Unfortunately, he does not name the woman religious he quotes.

20. McGreevy notes how these words became the most common declaration—almost a manifesto—for Catholic social activism during the decade of the sixties. See *Parish Boundaries*, 160. It is not too much to say that *Gaudium et spes* became a manifesto for Catholic social justice ministry in the United States.

People of God, are intimately bound up with all the concerns of those among whom we live."[21] Later, he would use this same sentiment to justify mandatory sermons on racial justice to be delivered in every Catholic parish after the major urban riots in 1967.

Thus *Gaudium et spes* both caused and justified a surge of Catholic involvement in U.S. peace and justice movements, both within the church and those of ecumenical or interfaith sponsorship. It is not an overstatement that because of *Gaudium et spes*, human rights ministries and commissions became considered to be essential ecclesial activities and legitimate expressions of faith. In the words of the later synodal document *Justice in the World* (1971), action for justice became a "constitutive dimension" of Catholic faith.

Gaudium et spes, then, created the breakthrough that enabled Catholic participation in what is arguably one of the most enduring social justice challenges that faced our nation. It is certainly the case that without *Gaudium et spes*, Catholic involvement in racial justice would have remained minimal, inadequate, and "embarrassing"—a legacy that honesty compels one to admit has not been entirely overcome.

Recent Tensions in the Reception of Gaudium et spes

The U.S. bishops' conference also engaged political and economic concerns with two landmark pastoral letters in the 1980s, one on war and one on the economy. The resulting documents "offered a moral vision that reflected Catholic social teaching coupled with more specific policy judgments, while acknowledging that these specific policy analyses did not carry the same authority as the broader moral teaching."[22] Women religious in the United States interpreted the "vision of solidarity central to *Gaudium et spes* as a mandate to serve disfranchised members of U.S. society and address pressing social needs of their day. In the 1970s and 1980s they began to work in a wide variety of social programs beyond those administered by Catholic institutions alone:

---

21. McGreevy, *Parish Boundaries*, 209-10.

22. Richard Gaillardetz, "Every Day the Church Should Give Birth to the Church," *National Catholic Reporter* (March 1, 2011), available at http://ncronline.org/news/faith-parish/every-day-church-should-give-birth-Church (accessed July 30, 2013).

in domestic violence shelters, educational programs for incarcerated women, addiction counseling centers, food banks and ecological justice programs. Beyond marching at Selma they witnessed in solidarity with striking farm workers and against nuclear proliferation. Tracing its roots to the Second Vatican Council, NETWORK social justice lobby's mission remains focused to this day upon closing the gap between rich and poor and dismantling policies rooted in racism, greed, and violence.

The year 2011 marked the twenty-fifth anniversary of "Economic Justice for All," but the U.S. bishops did not commemorate the event. In an op-ed in *The Baltimore Sun* that month, a former top staff official at the bishops' conference wrote: "I fear the Church's revered social justice witness is being crowded out by divisive culture-war battles at a time when Americans need a stronger moral message about the dignity of work and economic justice for all." Others insisted that the bishops' ongoing advocacy on economic issues—as founding members of the "Circle of Protection" movement to protect the poor and vulnerable in the federal budget, for example—are simply ignored by the media. Yet while a proposal was floated to raise domestic and international economic justice as a top conference priority at that November's meeting of the bishops, the suggestion was "tabled in favor of two other priorities: promoting a 'new evangelization' and defending religious freedom from the encroaching threats of same-sex marriage and insurance mandates to provide [contraception] to employees."[23]

Different interpretations of Vatican II in part account for these shifts in recent decades. An honest commemoration of *Gaudium et spes* and engagement with its legacy must take note of its contentious reception in the recent life of the church. By this, we mean a candid acknowledgment of significant tensions between not only the text of the conciliar document and more recent ecclesial statements, especially beginning with the pontificate of John Paul II in 1978, but also in the divergent visions of church that they express. We

---

23. David Gibson, "Bishops Quiet on Economic Turmoil 25 Years after Landmark Statement" (November 15, 2011), available at http://www.huffingtonpost.com/2011/11/15/bishops-silent-on-economic-turmoil_n_1095747.html (accessed July 29, 2013).

highlight three such areas of significant difference in vision, tone, and practice:

1. *The view of magisterial competence. Gaudium et spes* stressed the limited competence of church leaders in the life of the church and society. There is a humility in the description of church leadership that leads to a recognition of the need for a greater role for the laity and a shared sense of responsibility for the development of ecclesial and social life: "Let the [laity] not imagine that [their] pastors are always such experts that to every problem which arises, however complicated, they can give him a concrete solution, or event that such is their mission. . . . Let the laity take their distinctive role" (GS 43). A strikingly different, even contrary, stance is revealed in *Veritatis splendor*. Here, John Paul posits a magisterium that is extremely confident in its ability—almost in abstraction from the rest of the faith community—to know and teach moral truths even in the most difficult matters: "In addressing this Encyclical to you, my Brother Bishops, it is my intention to state the principles . . . [so that we can give] a reply that possesses a light and power capable of answering even the most controversial and complex questions" (VS 30). Thus in the recent life of the church we see a marked difference concerning the role and competence of the magisterium and the proper contribution of the lay faithful.

2. *The need for dialogue.* In *Gaudium et spes*, one finds a description of the entire people of God—including but not limited to Catholics—united in a global search for truth with other people of goodwill. Truth, both religious and moral, is not regarded as something already possessed but as a matter of ongoing and shared discovery: In fidelity to conscience, Christians are joined with the rest of men and women in the search for truth, and for the genuine solution to the numerous problems that arise in the life of individuals and from social relationships (GS 16). The vision of truth posited by John Paul is dramatically different. In *Veritatis splendor*, moral and religious truth is seen as something already in the possession of the magisterium, which is solely responsible for and capable of making it known to the rest of the church and, by implication, to the rest of humankind: "[In her moral teaching] the Magisterium does not bring to the Christian conscience truths which are extraneous to it; rather it brings to light the truths which it ought already to possess. . . . [Thus this teaching enables

"men"] especially in more difficult questions to attain the truth with certainty and to abide in it" (*VS* 64). The tension between seeing truth as something arrived at through common discernment with all people, including nonbelievers, and as a matter possessed principally (if not solely) by the magisterium, could not be more starkly evident.

Freedom of Theological Discussion and Inquiry
In keeping with the limited competence of church leaders to know the truth solely through their own efforts and their injunction to join with all of good will in the search for it, *Gaudium et spes* specially states the need for open and courageous dialogue within the church itself. Indeed, after expressing the hope that the lay faithful would become experts in the theological sciences, the Council declared: "Let it be recognized that all of the faithful, clerical and lay, possess a lawful freedom of inquiry and thought, and the freedom to express their minds humbly and courageously about those matters in which they enjoy competence" (*GS* 62).

One can argue that this bold declaration, rooted in a confidence in communal discernment, has been significantly eroded in the recent life of the church. Such a view stems from the long list of contemporary theologians who have been censured, disciplined, investigated, and/or silenced since 1978. The list includes reputable scholars such as Hans Küng, Charles Curran, André Guidon, Jacques Dupuis, Roger Haight, Jeannine Gramick, Robert Nugent, Leonardo Boff, Jon Sobrino, Marciano Vidal, John McNeill, Todd Salzman, Michael Lawler, Elizabeth Johnson, and Margaret Farley. Many of these have been censured or investigated for their views concerning official teachings on sexuality and gender. On such issues, above all, one sees major tensions between the "lawful freedom of inquiry and thought" envisioned by the Council and recent official church practices.

By no means are we contending that the pontificates of John Paul II and Benedict XVI mark a wholesale repudiation of or retreat from the vision enunciated in *Gaudium et spes*. Yet the fact of significant tensions and differences remains. Such neuralgic tensions point to unresolved issues that require continuing ecclesial discernment and development. Such unfinished and ongoing work is also part of the legacy of *Gaudium et spes*.

These tensions have played out in the U.S. context, where a new generation of young clerics who share John Paul II's high theology of the priesthood see in *Gaudium et spes* "a misplaced optimism in the possibility of constructive dialogue with the world," whereas they perceive "a world ensnared in a culture of death" marked by what Pope Benedict XVI called "the dictatorship of relativism." Hence in contrast to Cardinal Bernardin's "seamless garment," which presupposed the interconnectedness of Catholic teaching across a broad range of issues from abortion to euthanasia, the death penalty, concern for the poor, and the ethics of war (in the 1980s), a more countercultural mode that champions a more select moral agenda and construal of Catholic identity has been evident in the practices of withholding communion to Catholic politicians deemed insufficiently "pro-life" over the past three presidential election seasons; reaction to Notre Dame's decision to confer an honorary degree on President Obama; and the 2010 actions of the bishop of Phoenix who declared that St. Joseph's Hospital was no longer Catholic after doctors terminated a pregnancy to save a young woman's life.[24]

Case Study: The Affordable Care Act Controversy
Related questions of authority and conscience in public Catholicism came to the fore in the health care reform debate of 2010. Without delving into the details of the Affordable Care Act and its subsequent provisions, a brief overview of this question of the function of authority in today's church offers insights into these persistent tensions.[25] The later version of the Affordable Care Act was ultimately opposed by the U.S. bishops' conference and supported by the Catholic Health Association (CHA), NETWORK social justice lobby, and some congregations of women's religious. In the wake of their support of the health care reform bill, the motives and competencies of certain groups of women religious were impugned, with the USCCB issuing

---

24. See Gaillardetz, "Every Day the Church Should Give Birth," n. 23.

25. A fuller elaboration of different Catholic interpretations of the Affordable Care Act's passage appears in Kristin E. Heyer, "Reservoirs of Hope: Catholic Women's Witness," in *Women, Wisdom, Witness: Engaging Contexts in Conversation*, ed. Kathleen J. Dolphin and Rosemary P. Carbine (Collegeville, MN: Liturgical Press, 2012), 219-36.

an official statement charging "those who differed from the bishops' interpretation of the health care bill with causing confusion and a wound to Catholic unity."[26] Archbishop Charles Chaput accused the "self-described 'Catholic' groups" as committing "a serious disservice to justice, to the Church, and to the ethical needs of the American people by undercutting the leadership and witness of their own bishops."[27]

The focus in this fallout centered around the nature and limits of the bishops' authority on matters of faith, morals, law, and policy.[28] Important distinctions were revisited, such as the application of universal moral teachings and specific moral principles to concrete policies. Particular strategic *applications* of principles are more fluid in character, and hence our grasp is "necessarily more tentative than [our] knowledge of principle[s]." [29] In the case of the divergence of some women religious from the bishops on health care reform, the debate occurred nearly entirely at the level of prudential judgments about technical legislative language, not over the morality or legality of abortion per se.[30] By contrast, Cardinal Francis George, then president

---

26. Chairmen of USCCB committees on Pro-Life Activities, Immigration and Domestic Justice, Peace and Human Development, "Setting the Record Straight," May 21, 2010, available at http://www.usccb.org/comm/archives/2010/10-104.shtml (accessed October 8, 2010).

27. Archbishop Chaput, "A Bad Bill and How We Got It," *Denver Catholic Register* (March 24, 2010), available at http://www.archden.org/index.cfm/ID/3617/Archbishop's-Column/ (accessed March 2, 1014).

28. See Thomas Weinandy, OFM, Cap., "The Bishops and the Right Exercise of Authority," available at http://www.usccb.org/healthcare/11-01-10-commonweal-response.shtml (accessed April 27, 2011); John Allen, "Health Care: Transcript of Cardinal George June 16 NCR Interview," *National Catholic Reporter* (June 22, 2010), available at http://ncronline.org/blogs/ncr-today/health-care-transcript-cardinal-george-june-16-ncr-interview (accessed April 27, 2011); Daniel Finn, "Uncertainty Principle: The Bishops, Health Care & Prudence," *Commonweal* (March 25, 2011).

29. See Charles E. Curran, *Catholic Moral Tradition Today: A Synthesis* (Washington, DC: Georgetown University Press, 1999), 152n71.

30. Richard R. Gaillardetz, "The Limits of Authority: When Bishops Speak about Health Care Policy, Catholics Should Listen, But Don't Have to Agree," *Commonweal* (June 30, 2010): 9-11. The virtue of prudence is what helps guide the conscience in such practical moral judgments, including how citizens should

of the bishops' conference, cast the matter less in terms of pruden-tial judgment than the very nature of the church and its legitimate spokes(men).

The understanding of conscience articulated in *Gaudium et spes* is especially illuminating here.[31] Whereas an understanding of conscience as conformity to the teaching of the hierarchy remains in tension with the shift to a more personalist model at Vatican II, the discernment of Catholic groups at the health care reform moment demonstrates a response to the call to actively discern responsibility in light of the gift and challenge of God's law of love. As CHA President Sr. Carol Keehan put it, "This was a bill that, for the first time in the lives of 32 million Americans, gave them a chance to have decent health insurance.... That was a heavy burden on my conscience, and on our organizational conscience.... We did not differ on the moral question, or the teach-ing authority of the bishops."[32] In *Gaudium et spes*, the Council fathers characterize conscience as that "secret core and sanctuary of a person, where they are alone with God whose voice echoes in their depths." This "encounter with the divine basis of moral obligation is mediated through [a person's] agency, and hence through the spirit, reason, affec-tions and relationships that constitute human agency."[33]

---

vote. Attending to means, not ends, prudence carefully considers human expe-rience, others' counsel, anticipated consequences, and the discernment of God's invitation to reach a decision that best fits the complexities of a given situation. See Richard Gula, *Reason Informed by Faith: Foundations of Catholic Moral-ity* (Mahwah, NJ: Paulist Press, 1989), 316. Many rightly warn that appeals to prudence or conscience may too readily offer Catholics an easy "entrance to the cafeteria," yet genuinely wrestling with the tradition and its demands seems more reflective of the conciliar invitation than are impositions of control via loyalty oaths. The Council explicitly calls the church "to be a sign of that kinship which makes genuine dialogue possible and vigorous" (GS 92).

31. See Linda Hogan, *Confronting the Truth: Conscience in the Catholic Tradi-tion* (London: Darton, Longman & Todd, 2001).

32. John L. Allen, Jr., "Minding the Gap between the Bishops and Catho-lic Health Care," *National Catholic Reporter* (June 16, 2010), available at http://ncronline.org/news/politics/minding-gap-between-bishops-and-catholic-health-care (accessed October 8, 2010).

33. David E. DeCosse, "Conscience Issue Separates Catholic Moral Camps," *National Catholic Reporter* (November 10, 2009), available at http://ncronline.

The primacy of the human person is evident in the document's treatment of conscience, particularly in contrast to earlier emphases on moral norms as objective sources of morality. Moral manuals guided priests in the confessional where matters of conscience were assessed, resolved, and absolved from the sixteenth century to roughly the 1960s. The focus of concern was more often on conforming to rigors of church practices (fasting, abstinence) than facing challenges of living in the world, and confessors functioned as physicians of the soul who had the ability to discern right moral conduct for the penitent. But the Council shifted the focus to the role of conscience in discernment and execution of right moral action. For Bernard Häring (secretary of the editorial committee that drafted *Gaudium et spes*), conscience is rooted in freedom as the possibility of responding to God's call to do God's will, the power to do good.[34]

This conciliar understanding of conscience entails the capacity and willingness to pursue the truth about doing the right thing in concrete, complicated circumstances, rather than having all the answers.[35] Understanding conscientious discernment as inclusive of multiple sources of moral wisdom—including the riches of Scripture, the wisdom of the Catholic community over the centuries, natural law, insights of church officials and theologians, moral exemplars, as well as the reflective experiences of those immersed in health care ministries and the details of legislative analysis as in the case at hand—calls for a more complex and proactive endeavor than assumptions that restrict such sources to the teaching authority of the hierarchy alone.[36]

Thus, tensions between understanding freedom as the human person's most precious gift and the church as the only reliable interpreter of moral law *persist* amid fears not only that conscience becomes an excuse for doing whatever you want but, as in the health care case, fears that divergence from the conclusions of clearly established authorities

---

org/news/conscience-issue-separates-catholic-moral-camps (accessed March 2, 2014).

34. James F. Keenan, S.J., "Vatican II and Theological Ethics," *Theological Studies* 74 (2013): 162-90, at 165-66.

35. According to the Catholic tradition, conscience entails a three-part structure entailing conscience as innate capacity, process, and judgment.

36. DeCosse, "Conscience Issue."

confuses and gives "scandal." Taking to heart the conciliar recognition that "God's Spirit is given to all the faithful and not only to those in positions of hierarchical office" impacts one's understandings of conscience and authority.

In the aftermath of the health care act's passage, *New York Times* columnist Nicholas Kristof detailed accounts of the "two Catholic Churches" he encounters through his international travels: one the rigid, all-male, Vatican hierarchy obsessed with dogma and rules (that he deems "out of touch"), and the other, which supports life-saving aid organizations and operates "superb schools that provide needy children an escalator out of poverty." Kristof's bifurcated depiction may resonate with those who prefer to retreat to either the hierarchical or "grass-roots" versions.[37] Yet Richard Gaillardetz lifts up the unity of the faith that Catholics profess, concluding that there must arise a place where "the doctrinal teaching of the bishops and the dirt-stained testimony of those who experience God's grace on inner-city streets, in prisons and hospitals can meet."[38] In the spirit of *Gaudium et spes*, discerning the promptings of the Spirit in the church and the world demands that these different routes not only encounter but mutually inform each other.

These tensions between doctrinal orthodoxy and engagement in the social justice works of the church (or consultative listening to felt concerns of ordinary laypeople) need not be incommensurate per se, but they threaten to distract when they recur in the headlines particularly in terms of guilt by association. In the U.S. context critics have charged that some affiliations of Catholic groups (e.g., the domestic anti-poverty grants of the Catholic Campaign for Human Development and the development work of Catholic Relief Services) undermine the teaching of the bishops (often related to family planning support as part of partner organizations' anti-poverty and gender justice

37. Nicholas Kristof, "A Church Mary Can Love," *New York Times* (April 18, 2010).

38. Thomas C. Fox, "Women Religious Experiences Have Implications for Entire Church" (August 12, 2010), available at http://ncronline.org/news/women-religious/women-religious-experiences-have-implications-entire-Church (accessed September 1, 2010).

efforts). By contrast the scandal emphasized in *Gaudium et spes* concerns polarizing economic and social differences: "For excessive economic and social differences between the members of the one human family or population groups cause scandal, and militate against social justice, equity, the dignity of the human person, as well as social and international peace."[39]

The Promise of *Gaudium et spes* Today and the Ministry of Pope Francis

Discerning the prospects for cultivating the promise of *Gaudium et spes* in our day requires learning from both challenges and signs of hope that have marked these past fifty years. Engaging complex social realities "on the ground" may help to redress the disconnect between top-down, centralized practices and the church's public advocacy of dialogue, grassroots engagement, and human rights. By way of one example, the binational Kino Border Initiative (KBI) operates in Ambos Nogales at the Mexico-Arizona border. During the KBI's painstakingly extensive needs-assessment phase, discussions with many individuals on both the Mexican and U.S. sides of the border alerted them to pressing needs: the vulnerability of women on the move and the intransigence of immigration attitudes close to the border. As a result, KBI focused its initial programming to meet these felt concerns (rather than simply sending a Jesuit in to staff a parish there as was initially requested). KBI explicitly understands itself as operating with one foot on either side of the border, as "a point of mutual transformation not only for the migrant community members who encounter one another in the context of [its] programs, but also for the [Jesuit] Provinces of California and Mexico, the Missionary Sisters of the Eucharist, and Jesuit Refugee Services."[40] This posture reflects a "two-way street" of social engagement, modeling partnership and reciprocal "evangelization" in the spirit of *Gaudium et spes*. In this vein Catholic social action can remain open to ongoing conversion by

---

39. GS 29.

40. Mark W. Potter, "Solidarity as Spiritual Exercise: Accompanying Migrants at the US/Mexico border," *Political Theology* 12.6 (2011): 830-42, at 842.

the suffering and resilience of those in need, rather than triumphalistic in its possession of truth or static in its formulations.

Moving forward, the continuing reception and impact of *Gaudium et spes* for social justice praxis in the United States will undoubtedly be decisively influenced by the ministry and teaching of Pope Francis. As we write this, Francis's pontificate is less than a year old. It is too soon to tell what his influence will be. However, we can see in his interventions thus far signs that signal a recovery of the major themes that mark this document.

For example, while not at all calling for changes in the church's doctrinal teachings on abortion and homosexuality, Francis has signaled that these should not be the leading issues that mark Catholic presence in the public square. Certainly, one cannot read Francis as supporting that these are "the Catholic issues" that constitute a kind of "litmus test," as some U.S. conservative activist groups—and a few bishops—maintain. Francis writes:

> The message we preach runs a greater risk of being distorted or reduced to some of its secondary aspects. In this way certain issues which are part of the Church's moral teaching are taken out of the context which gives them their meaning. The biggest problem is when the message we preach then seems identified with those secondary aspects which, important as they are, do not in and of themselves convey the heart of Christ's message. (*Evangelii gaudium*, 34)

Rather, in continuity with *Gaudium et spes*, we see a constant refrain in many of Francis's interventions that the Catholic faith community is to be a poor church that acts decisively on behalf of the poor out of a life shared with the poor (*Evangelii gaudium*, 198). As *Evangelii gaudium* states:

> The Gospel tells us constantly to run the risk of a face-to-face encounter with others, with their physical presence which challenges us, with their pain and their pleas, with their joy which infects us in our close and continuous interaction. True faith in the incarnate Son of God is inseparable from self-giving, from membership in the community, from service, from reconciliation

with others. The Son of God, by becoming flesh, summoned us to the revolution of tenderness (88).

Finally, one can point to his call for broader consultation of the faithful in preparation for the upcoming synod on the family to be held in the fall of 2014. In a move that is without precedent, episcopal conferences were mandated to inquire among their people concerning Catholic attitudes toward and reception of a range of church teachings and issues, including the neuralgic issues of birth control, the treatment of the divorced and remarried, and the pastoral care of same-sex parented families. Here we can discern a retrieval of Vatican II's insight that the church is the entire people of God, not simply the hierarchy. Indeed, in his landmark interview published in leading Jesuit global periodicals, Francis declares, "Thinking with the Church does not mean thinking only with the hierarchy of the Church."

In short, it is far too soon to tell how this pontificate will influence the future reception of *Gaudium et spes* in the United States. We can be confident, however, that Francis's ministry will undoubtedly rekindle new interest in this document—and be hopeful that it will mark a renewed commitment to being a church more and more in tune with the voices of joy and anguish present among the poor and afflicted in our nation.

7

Locked Together in (Religious) Argument

Justifying Vatican II's Declaration on Religious Liberty

J. LEON HOOPER, S.J.

Between the third and the fourth sessions of Vatican II (on November 28, 1964), the American Jesuit John Courtney Murray had the following to say about a draft of what became the conciliar Declaration on Religious Liberty[1] (*Dignitatis humanae personae* [*DH*]), more specifically about the fourth draft for which Murray was the "first scribe":[2]

---

1. Throughout most of this discussion, the term "religious liberty" designates a civil or civic institution, that is, a coercive law enforcing a political immunity (thus my use of the phrase "civil liberty" is a redundancy for the sake of emphasis). "Religious freedom" concerns much, much more, but is mentioned only toward the end of this article.

2. The third conciliar period closed on November 21, 1964. Earlier in that period, Alfredo Cardinal Ottaviani had blocked public discussion of the fourth (Murray's) draft. Murray's talk quoted here was delivered during the interperiod at Georgetown University, Washington, DC. During the fourth period (September 14–December 8, 1965), religious liberty was taken up, culminating in the approval of a final draft of *DH* on December 7, 1965. For a discussion of the generation of *DH*, see Donald E. Pelotte, *John Courtney Murray: Theologian in Conflict* (New York: Paulist Press, 1976), 74-114. For an outline of the full development of Murray's argument, see my General Introduction to John Courtney Murray, *Religious Liberty: Catholic Struggles with Pluralism* (Louisville, KY: Westminster/John Knox, 1993), 11-48.

Religious freedom today is not based on—or certainly not necessarily based on—any irreligious ideology, as was the case in
the nineteenth century. And that introduces an historical question. Oh, this historical question! I wrote it five different times
and it's still no good. . . . It undertakes to make just one point,
namely, you have the fact that Pius IX, exactly a hundred years
before *Pacem in terris*, said exactly the opposite to what John
XXIII said. Pius IX, quoting Gregory XVI, said that religious freedom is a nightmare, a *deliramentum*, such a fantasy as
might overcome a man in the middle of the night. An illusion.
John XXIII exactly a hundred years later says that religious
freedom is a natural right of man. A man has a right to worship God according to the dictates of his conscience. Well, this
presents a nice little problem in the development of doctrine.
How do you get two popes who say exactly the opposite things
to be really saying the same thing? Well, this is what we have
theologians for.[3]

As it turned out, Murray's humorous confidence in the future of
his own argument/draft for civil religious liberty proved premature.
When first I studied Murray, I was puzzled by his late-fourth-period
and postconciliar claims that what we must affirm as magisterial is
Dignitatis's unequivocally affirmative judgment on the goodness or
correctness of religious liberty, not any of the arguments that *Dignitatis* advanced for that affirmation.[4] Read even fifty years after the
Council, Murray appears to be denying his own baby. Here I first
want to determine whose baby *Dignitatis* was and, then, what was
and is at stake in our uneven reception of the document. In the process I discuss not only the reception but also the genesis of religious
liberty as an essential institution for our large-scale civil and ecclesial
living.

---

3. This is a partial transcription of an audio tape, found in the Murray
Archives, Georgetown University Special Collections, box 7, files 520-22.

4. For example, see Murray's commentary in *The Documents of Vatican II*,
ed. Walter H. Abbott, S.J. (New York: Herder & Herder, 1966), 672–96, esp.
680n7.

Three Fifty-Year-Old Bridges

During the formation of *Dignitatis*, Murray described three justifi-cations for the church's possible acceptance of civil religious liberty, three distinct arguments to bridge the counterclaims of Pius IX and John XXIII.[5] That which he called the "First View"—in contrast to the "Second" and the "French" views—understood religious liberty to be at all times and in all places an intrinsic evil, as against God's will and hopes for civic and ecclesial living. Yet, while the institu-tion itself is always evil, settling for religious liberty might not be immoral or irreligious. Catholics can and must, at times, live and cooperate with religious liberty as the lesser of two evils. In this reading, John XXIII's endorsement, in the face of rampant twen-tieth-century individualism and pluralism, was a legitimate way to avoid, say, outright civil anarchy.

The Second and the French views each affirmed that religious liberty is a moral (and perhaps religious) good, but differed con-cerning the social source of that good. The Second View, which was Murray's argument for which in 1953 he was silenced, insisted that the insight into and commitment to the moral (and religious) good-ness of religious liberty arose first outside the church, from within a mostly Anglo-American tradition of social ethical reflection. Admit-tedly, modernity's new insight and judgment were often opposed by the church, but, Murray argued, modernity has in fact revealed a new moral truth, placing a moral obligation on the church.

The third bridging argument, the French View, had little sympathy for the Anglo-American emergence that Murray claimed for religious liberty. This argument judged that civic religious liberty is a moral and (perhaps) religious good, but found its social and historical roots in early Christian sources, not, as did Murray, in a convergence of reli-gious and secular arguments, expressed—or revealed—by the signs of our own times. Briefly put, then, Murray found the specific good

---

5. The discussion in this section is taken from John Courtney Murray, *The Problem of Religious Freedom* (Westminster, MD: Newman, 1964). Earlier versions were published by the conciliar documentation service. Most Murray materials can be accessed at http://woodstock.georgetown.edu/library/Murray/0_murraybib.html.

of civil religious liberty revealed first outside the church; the French found it first within the (earliest if later forgetful) church.

Which of these three justifications is dominant in *Dignitatis* and what is the relationship between the three? It appears that the attempt to found religious liberty on early Christian sources was *Dignitatis's* primary argument and that others, including Murray's, were last minute additions to an essentially French text.[6] What, then, can we "receive" in *Dignitatis?* Wherever one finds an insistence that we must search for the truth and adhere to that truth when found, one is dealing with the argument that for centuries had allowed Catholics to coexist with religious liberty as a lesser of two evils (and to coerce when opportune). Again, wherever one finds modern juridical notions, particularly the principle of "as much freedom as possible, as much coercion as necessary," or theological admissions that the church as an institution has sinned by coercively restraining religiously heterodox public proclamations, one is encountering Murray's own justification for religious liberty as a historically emergent moral and religious good. And where one finds attempts to found civil religious liberty in Scripture or the suggestion that the early church actually favored civil liberty, one is reading the French argument. These three arguments are not linked in the final declaration; their mutual contraries and contradictions remain unaddressed. The French argument dominates mostly by quantity and its ability to highlight the best of then-current Roman Catholic political intentions.

So, then, conservative scholars can and have claimed that the last minute insertion of the lesser-of-two-evils argument was a repudiation of both the French and especially the Second views.[7] And such

---

6. Space does not allow a discussion how this happened. It had to do with when Murray's lung collapsed and with Paul VI's upcoming talk at the United Nations. In the face of the latter, even the final seventy votes against the ultimate draft of *DH* were something of an embarrassment. The mid-200 negative votes (out of 2,300) that Murray's texts evoked approached the scandalous. The strategy of giving something to everyone helped the vote count (a good thing, actually) while it left many loose ends.

7. Very good at arguing for a First View reading of *DH* is David L. Schindler, "Editorial: The Repressive Logic of Liberal Rights: Religious Freedom, Contraceptives, and the 'Phony' Argument of the New York Times," *Communio* (Winter 2011): 523-47.

claims for an ongoing priority of the First View have been encouraged by John Paul II's and particularly Benedict XVI's challenges to any notion of substantive discontinuity between the teachings of Vatican I and Vatican II, a discontinuity that is core to Murray's reading not only of *Dignitatis* but also of the other two conciliar documents that look outward for redeeming grace, namely, *Nostra aetate* and *Gaudium et spes.*

Current Retakes of the Three Bridges

The best contemporary readings of *DH*—by John O'Malley and scholars of the University of Bologna[8]—themselves distinguish three justifications, now labeled *aggiornamento*, development, and *ressourcement.* Each comes in weak and in strong forms.[9]

The first bridging is spun from John XXIII's preconciliar call for *aggiornamento.* In its weakest form, it allows that at times we must live with less-than-desirable institutions; that is, it allows for a lesser-of-two-evils argument. Other forms of *aggiornamento* allow that goods have developed outside the church to which the church ought to be attentive. These goods can range from the material, to technological, to cultural, to moral, and/or to religious. These understandings of *aggiornamento* become stronger as one allows for more types of externally emergent goods, moving from the material to the religious. While most believers are only moderate *aggiornamentoists*, claiming for themselves privileged and closed moral or especially religious insight, there are conceivably stronger forms of *aggiornamento* that are more willing to notice even novel and important religious goods emerging outside their immediate religious communions. In my judgment, this

8. In what follows, I rely mostly on, and spar with, John W. O'Malley's *What Happened at Vatican II* (Cambridge, MA: Belknap Press of Harvard University Press, 2008), and his "'The Hermeneutic of Reform': A Historical Analysis," *Theological Studies* 73 (September 2012): 517-43.

9. As best I know, O'Malley first mentioned the possibility of strong and weak variations (only in relation to the notion of "development") at a 2012 talk at Georgetown University in his response to a question concerning the possibility of the church learning from outside its own institutional boundaries. Here I have expanded that notion to encompass all three understandings of reforming the tradition.

strongest type of *aggiornamento* was at play in the difference between French and Anglo-American attempts to found religious liberty.

O'Malley presents Mariology, articulated in the nineteenth-century doctrine of the Assumption and the twentieth-century definition of the Immaculate Conception, as a paradigm of a strong (conservative) notion of development. Here development is thought to be cumulative and increasingly more specific. Vatican I's affirmation of papal infallibility is also thought to be a development and a deepening specification from which we cannot back away. Here a truth not found in the founding religious experience could conceivably emerge from outside the tradition. Given, however, the conservative Catholic examples that O'Malley offers, his presentation does not explore possible challenges posed by novel developments sourced outside the Catholic tradition.

O'Malley's final theological means for bridging gaps in papal teaching is *ressourcement*—the return from later historical accretions and distortions to the original, allegedly purer sources of one's faith, its beginnings in Scripture and the Fathers of the Church. Here it is recognized that some developments in church teaching can be time-limited, incorrect, and perhaps even sinful (in stronger versions of this theory). Nonetheless, the truth of what constitutes followers of Christ is thought to be contained in those early resources, completely if inchoately (thus presuming that at some past moment revelation has been definitively and finally presented).

Some charge that Murray was silenced mostly for his arrogance or because of Rome's ignorance. But in fact, Ottaviani and other conservative Catholics well understood that Murray was making an uncomfortable ecclesial claim, namely, that God can speak a new truth to believers out of the mouth of the heretical or even atheistic ass. The elision over this possibility in O'Malley's study removes an at least interesting tool (that is, the notion that God has something new to reveal to both us and the Other) in our contemporary approaches to interreligious collaboration.

Modernity's Novel Good

What was that good that was developed outside the Roman Catholic Church, at least according to some who voted for Murray's fourth draft as the received text? Certainly it was civil religious liberty as a constitutional institution, which in the United States and elsewhere was proving beneficial to the church. But it was much more than a simple juridical structuring. That which was being learned from the secular world was the necessity, for large-scale social living, of distinctively new virtues and social relationships. As Murray studied Western constitutional history, he insisted that the Anglo-American political tradition was based on a "great act of faith" in the moral agency of the people, which he further tried to explicate as itself deeply grounded in the Thomistic claim that the justice of the king is to be authenticated not by the king nor by elites, not by scholars nor by the church. The liberal traditions of the West, he claimed, recognized the moral agency of the people as the forum, source, and adjudicator of governmental justice, eventually bringing such claims to constitutional expression. This, Murray continued with fragile appeals to Pope Pius XII, [10] was a new moral insight now being recognized by the church in the face of the early twentieth-century rise of Fascism and Communism. The institution and the ongoing moral action of peoples were newly recognized as according to the will of Nature's God. And this new will lays inescapable moral and religious demands on religious believers, including Roman Catholics—claims that were not available to the early church and therefore not derivative solely from that early church.

Beyond the state and the institutional church now stood the people, in one of Murray's favorite phrases, permanently locked together in moral and religious argument. The heart of the common good had become the conversing itself. It was an ongoing action, a verb, foundational to but distinct from all the other public, much less private, goods we pursue. The common good of Catholic social thought is an ongoing acting that must be maintained in act. To hinder the conversing is a direct assault on the common good.

---

10. In a Christmas address in 1944, Pius XII had declared that democracy was "a postulate of nature imposed by reason itself." This was a form of natural law thinking that necessarily also included a natural theology. Once Murray and others situated natural law and its accompanying natural theology within history, they could entertain the possibility of new religious, not simply moral, truths emerging beyond the boundaries of the church.

But what does a society locked together in argument look like? A few twists that Murray himself had to undergo can be instructive. Again, good soldier that he was, Murray worked with just about every conservative Catholic argument he could find until they disintegrated in his hands. For example, for most of his life he had claimed that strictly theological talk between Catholics and other Christians was impossible, that we must restrict our ecumenical conversations to natural law and Nature's God. But after the Council, Murray argued Bernard Lonergan's notion of trinitarian doctrine with Lutherans and issues of ecclesiastical discipline, liberty, and freedom with Anglicans. Again, for all but his last four years he had insisted that no Christian could deal with communists except in the forceful politics of *Realpolitik*. There did not exist, he judged, any common ground with atheists (neither even Nature nor Nature's God) on which to understand each other. But then, after the Council, albeit with some twisting and screaming, he began talking with Marxists and atheistic existentialists about our mutual *gnosis* (knowledge) and our *agnosis* (ignorance) of God.[11] Being locked together in the difficult twists of transparent conversation became the public good to be acknowledged in the signs of his own times and practiced out of and within his own religious faith. And he expected his church also to learn and practice those transparent but difficult discussions that large-scale social living, ecclesial and civic, newly demands.

At issue is a virtue or set of virtues (and vices) that we are only now beginning to understand. The virtues, however, did earlier surface in Murray's discussions of what is needed in public education for the proper moral functioning of We the People. There, the Murray who had earlier claimed that we had best avoid external talking about the revealed foundations of our own Catholic faith now argued that all faiths should be taught in public schools, preferably by believers.[12] He was not asking for proselytizing. He wanted students to be able to

---

11. John Courtney Murray, *The Problem of God, Yesterday and Today* (New Haven, CT: Yale University Press, 1964): 101-21.

12. John Courtney Murray, "Creeds at War Intelligibly," in *We Hold These Truths: Catholic Reflections on the American Proposition* (New York: Sheed & Ward, 1960), 125-39.

notice the links between the core commitments of a faith community and that community's policy recommendations. For example, if we Catholics claim to support religious liberty, we are under obligation to demonstrate how that support is anchored in our deepest faith commitments, and Protestants have a right to know how those commitments are so linked.

Why? For the sake of public trust. If I cannot demonstrate such links, then those outside my religious community will have to live with the possibility, as will I, that there might come a time when I must coercively suppress their public voices. Integrity demands public transparency. Transparency *can* encourage integrity. Thus the need for well-argued, postconciliar justifications for religious liberty.

It is this set of virtues, I think, that can best ground the third of the "issues behind the issues" that O'Malley identifies as at the core of Vatican II as a social language event. In O'Malley's telling, these three issues or trajectories are (1) historicity, (2) the relationship of the societal centers and peripheries, and (3) the question of "style." The new "style" of conciliar interactions can be understood as the emergence of a genuinely new arena of ethical living, at best analogous (i.e., "partly the same but entirely different") to smaller-scale living. At first reading, Murray's dynamic public transparency or O'Malley's new "style" can appear to be simple interpersonal niceties added as a frosting to our ethical or religious cake, a bit of human kindness—or even maybe the interpersonal kindness of Jesus[13]—smoothing slightly the sharp edges of national and international necessity. However, if Murray is right, the requirements for this transparent arguing or "style" emerge internally to modern, large-scale social living, not as external additions. Transparent conversing is a core requirement for the moral functioning of social realities that are beyond the reach of interpersonal bonds. It is demanded by Nature and Nature's God.

---

13. Some readings of Pope Francis's acting in church and society, as well as much of his *Evangelii gaudium*, can be so interpreted as practicing an interpersonal kindness of Jesus, whereas his refusal to let go those with whom he disagrees, as well as Jesus's own behavior, certainly more coherently matches the notions of "style" or argument discussed here.

Religious Liberty and Freedom on the Ground

And it is here that Murray's claims and our present ecclesial reality become difficult and challenging. Integrity and honesty demand that we (whether popes or pick-and-choose Catholics) admit that we have not been locking together in argument concerning many contemporary moral or theological issues. We sometimes know how to proclaim but not how to argue with style. Proclamation as assertion of judgments, no matter how gentle, is not argument. If there is, as Murray insisted, this new, modern realm of ethical acting that places legitimate and godly demands on us, then the current church appears to be immoral in two specific regards.

First, by not encouraging internal church argument on a full range of theological and ethical topics, we are demonstrating—to those outside the church and to our own young—that we choose not to operate by social-communicative norms that postmodern worlds are discovering to be necessary for their moral functioning. To suppress argument over links between our theology and our policy assertions is by contemporary standards immoral in a way that it was not in the tenth century. And, second, by engaging in external, civic conversations at most only by way of proclamation, we are similarly discouraging an activity that is our civic common good. By not living by O'Malley's "style" or Murray's argument, we can be reasonably judged to be bent on killing that distinct social good that modernity has revealed. Murray called such a refusal a "tribalism." It proclaims that our God is smarter, or more loving, or more revealing than is your God, but it demonstrates publicly little of that God's wisdom, or love, or self-giving.

At their core, the possible manners of understanding the gaps that opened up at Vatican II are matters of faith: Is our God capable of giving God's self to us, capable of revealing something new to us even from outside our tradition? The revelation we need, like the needs themselves, are sometimes new and distinct; they were not available to our founding generations. Murray's final justification for religious liberty (now fully "freedom" as empowerment) was the need for God's active grace in every human construct into which our science and technology propel us.

It is a truism that the Catholic Church in the United States has moved from large-scale public debates on peace and nuclear weapons, on the economy, on the position of women in the church and society, to a stance of public proclamation that forgoes the discipline of being locked together in argument. Proclamation actually makes far fewer demands on religious freedom than does involvement in argument; it requires only a personal immunity—having one's voice not silenced. It is, then, not surprising that our episcopal appeals to the right of religious liberty call upon merely the most individualistic and privatized notions of a human right as our most vehemently anti-Western Catholics insist.[14] It ought to strike believers who have stood strongly against Western individualism and the privatizing of religion as something of a tragedy that we can do no better. But, again, to do better would be to take risks that there is more to be revealed and that there is a God capable now of participating in that revealing and in our mutual reform.

---

14. Ad Hoc Committee for Religious Liberty, United States Conference of Catholic Bishops, "Our First, Most Cherished Liberty: A Statement on Religious Liberty," *Origins: CNS Documentary Service* 41/46 (April 26, 2012). This argument is developed mostly by Archbishop William E. Lori.

8

Soteriological Agnosticism
and Interreligious Dialogue

CATHERINE CORNILLE

Much of the discussion in the discipline of theology of religions since Vatican II has focused on the question of the salvation of non-Christians, and in particular on the status of non-Christian religions as mediators of salvation. This is not surprising considering the centrality of soteriology in Christian thought and practice. And the history of Christian attitudes toward other religions prior to Vatican II has tended to focus on Cyprian's warning that "there is no salvation outside the church."[1] As such, the value of non-Christian religions has been and continues to be assessed according to blanket and a priori judgments of their salvific power.

One of the remarkable features of Vatican II, however, is that it refrains from general pronouncements on the salvific value of non-Christian religions. This silence has nevertheless led to widespread speculation on the intended or the implicit view of the salvific status of other religions, informing the classical paradigms of exclusivism, inclusivism, and pluralism. The discussion around the role of other religions in the process of salvation seems to have reached something of an impasse, with different theological positions firmly entrenched, and their implications for interreligious dialogue narrowly defined. In order to move beyond the impasse, I suggest that we return to the

---

1. As many have pointed out, this third-century expression was originally not directed to non-Christians but rather to heretics and schismatics within the church. For a helpful overview of the history of the adage, see Gavin D'Costa, "'Extra ecclesiam nulla salus' Revisited," in *Religious Pluralism and Unbelief*, ed. Ian Hamnett (London: Routledge, 1990), 130-47.

silence or agnosticism of the Vatican II documents with regard to the salvific status of other religions and focus instead on the epistemological questions regarding the nature and status of truth in other religions, which *are* discussed in the documents, and on their import for the dialogue between religions.

Salvation outside the Church

There is little doubt or disagreement about the fact that the Vatican II documents affirm the possibility of salvation outside the church. *Lumen gentium* 16 states emphatically that

> those also can attain to salvation who through no fault of their own do not know the Gospel of Christ or His Church, yet sincerely seek God and moved by grace strive by their deeds to do His will as it is known to them through the dictates of conscience.

There is some debate over whether or not this represents a change in the attitude of the church toward non-Christians. While it seems to suggest a radical departure from the traditional adage *extra ecclesiam nulla salus*, the church has for centuries allowed for exceptions to this rule, and came to actually condemn individuals (such as Leonard Feeney, S.J.) who came to apply the expression in terms too rigid and literal. The Council of Trent (1545-1563) already recognized the possibility of a "baptism of desire" for those who lived a life of holiness without having received actual baptism, and in the document *Singulari quodam* (1854), Pope Pius IX officially speaks of the reality of "invincible ignorance," thereby de-culpabilizing those who through no fault of their own had never been exposed to the truth of the gospel. Hence, one might say that, though the possibility of the salvation of non-Christians was not previously denied, it is only in the documents of Vatican II that it was positively and formally affirmed with what Jacques Dupuis calls "unprecedented assurance."[2] This affirmation was itself of course the fruit of considerable prior theological reflection and debate in which theologians such as Karl Rahner and Hans

---

2. Jacques Dupuis, *Toward a Christian Theology of Religious Pluralism* (Maryknoll, NY: Orbis Books, 1997), 161.

Urs von Balthasar played an important role. Rahner himself referred to the optimism concerning salvation as "one of the most noteworthy results of the Second Vatican Council."[3]

While most Catholic theologians have welcomed and applauded the attitude of openness and generosity with regard to the salvation of non-Christians,[4] some have been more guarded or apprehensive about a purely optimistic interpretation of the documents of Vatican II regarding the salvation of non-Christians. This apprehension is mainly informed by a concern for the missionary mandate of the church. In his book *Will Many Be Saved?* Ralph Martin, for example, calls attention to the fact that the text from *Lumen gentium* 16, which affirms the possibility of salvation of all, is immediately qualified by the warning:

> But often men, deceived by the Evil One, have become vain in their reasonings and have exchanged the truth of God for a lie, serving the creature rather than the Creator. Or some there are who, living and dying in this world without God, are exposed to final despair. Wherefore to promote the glory of God and procure the salvation of all of these, and mindful of the command of the Lord, "Preach the Gospel to every creature," the Church fosters the missions with care and attention.

This passage, Martin believes, undercuts or at least strongly nuances the earlier positive statements in that "'very often' human beings are not living their lives in a way that will lead them to salvation, and there is a real possibility of many being lost unless they are addressed with a call to repentance, faith, and baptism."[5] For Martin, it is the omission of the biblical teaching on sin that has stemmed or even halted the missionary zeal of the church and that "needs to be corrected if

---

3. Karl Rahner, "Observations on the Problem of the 'Anonymous Christian,'" in *Theological Investigations*, vol. 14 (New York: Seabury, 1976), 284.

4. See in particular Gerald O'Collins's very helpful survey of biblical sources supporting the belief in the possibility of universal salvation: *Salvation for All God's Other Peoples* (Oxford: Oxford University Press, 2008).

5. Ralph Martin, *Will Many Be Saved? What Vatican II Actually Teaches and Its Implications for the New Evangelization* (Grand Rapids, MI: Eerdmans, 2012), 131-32.

the urgent call for a new evangelization is to achieve its considerable promise."[6]

Though this call to a more nuanced or cautious understanding of the possibility of salvation outside the church has its supporters,[7] the overall message from the documents is that God's salvific grace is also at work outside the church. The difference between being inside and being outside the church is succinctly captured by Wayne Teasdale when he states that "*Nostra aetate* has an optimism about salvation outside the church but a certainty of salvation within."[8]

Salvation and the Religions

All of this leaves open the question of the role of other religions in the salvation of their followers. Do these religions play a positive and constitutive role in the process of salvation, or are non-Christians saved in spite of their religious traditions? The documents of Vatican II are remarkably silent on this point. They speak in very positive terms about other religions in general and about certain religions in particular. *Nostra aetate*, while originally intended to correct distorted views of Jews and Judaism, also came to include positive statements about Islam, Hinduism, Buddhism, and other religions that "attempt in their own ways to calm the hearts of men by outlining a program of life covering doctrine, moral precepts and sacred rites"(2). The text continues by stating that "The Catholic Church rejects nothing of what is true and holy in these religions. She has a high regard for the manner of life and conduct, the precepts and doctrines which, although differing in many ways from her own teaching, nevertheless often reflect a ray of that truth which enlightens all men." *Lumen gentium* 16 speaks even more explicitly of "the plan of salvation," which includes "that people to which the covenants and the promises were made, and from which Christ was born in the flesh," "those who acknowledge the Creator, in the first place amongst whom are the Moslems," and "those who in shadows and images seek the unknown God." But the documents stop

---

6. Ibid., 208.

7. The book was endorsed by a good number of American bishops.

8. Wayne Teasdale, *Catholicism in Dialogue* (London: Rowman & Littlefield, 2004), 63.

short of explicitly recognizing these religions as "ways of salvation." This silence of the documents of Vatican II on the salvific role of other religions has opened the door to radically different interpretations. Some, such as Gerald O'Collins, suggest that the documents implicitly affirm other religions as ways to salvation:

> To be sure, the Council does not expressly speak of "ways of revelation and salvation," but what it says of Islam and, to a lesser extent, Hinduism, Buddhism, and other religions, amounts to recognizing them to be such "ways" to God.[9]

He qualifies this by saying that this does not mean that other religions are equal or complete ways to salvation, independent or unrelated to the church. But it is through, and not in spite of, their beliefs and practices that these non-Christians are brought closer to God.[10] Jacques Dupuis states a little more cautiously that "Even while much of what the Council affirms inclines toward the positive statement, the conclusions are not firmly drawn."[11] Others, such as Gavin D'Costa, have interpreted the silence of the documents as an implicit "refusal to acknowledge other religions, *per se*, as possibly being salvific structures."[12] He states that "it may well be the case that the documents' silences are intentional and could be read, as I would suggest, as prohibiting any unqualified positive affirmation of other religions as salvific structures, or as containing divine revelation."[13] D'Costa thus interprets the absence of explicit acknowledgment of other religions as

---

9. Gerald O'Collins, *The Second Vatican Council on Other Religions* (Oxford: Oxford University Press, 2013), 163.

10. Other theologians arguing for a recognition of other religions as ways of salvation are Piero Rossano in his article in the volume *Christ's Lordship and Religious Pluralism*, ed. Gerald Anderson and Thomas Stransky (Maryknoll, NY: Orbis Books, 1981), 102-3; and K. Kunnumpuram, *Ways of Salvation: The Salvific Meaning of Non-Christian Religions according to the Teaching of Vatican II* (Poona: Pontifical Atheneum, 1971).

11. Jacques Dupuis, *Toward a Christian Theology of Religious Pluralism* (Maryknoll, NY: Orbis Books, 1997), 169.

12. Gavin D'Costa, *The Meeting of Religions and the Trinity* (Maryknoll, NY: Orbis Books, 2000), 109.

13. Ibid., 105.

ways of salvation as an implicit negation.[14] This interpretation could be inferred from the fact that the Council, while in many respects inspired by the theology of Karl Rahner, did not follow him in referring to other religions as "lawful" and as "a positive means for gaining the right relationship to God and thus for the attaining of salvation, a means which is therefore positively included in God's plan of salvation."[15] Paul Knitter, for example, makes much of the fact that the Council "did not follow Rahner in expressly concluding that the religions are to be viewed as possible, or probably, 'ways of salvation'— instruments by which God draws people to God's self."[16]

In all this history and development of theological reflection, little or no attention has been paid to the theological significance of the *silence* of the Vatican II documents on the question of the salvific role of non-Christian religions. Knitter admits that the bishops "neither affirmed nor denied that the religions might be actual conduits by which the Spirit flows into the lives of people beyond the Church" and acknowledges that "perhaps the reason they didn't decide this question was that they deliberately chose not to."[17] He suggests that this choice may have been informed by the style and intention of the Council, which was pastoral, rather than doctrinal. However, I wish to propose that there may also be deeper theological insight and wisdom, whether conscious or not, in refraining from passing judgment on the salvific status of other religions.

Soteriological Agnosticism

There are many sound theological and philosophical reasons for practicing a form of agnosticism with regard to the soteriological function of other religions. From a purely existential perspective, one might first

---

14. Other theologians arguing that the texts deny salvific value to other religions are Paul Hacker, *Theological Foundations of Evangelization* (St. Augustin: Steyler Verlag, 1980), 61-77; and Ralph Martin, *Will Many Be Saved?* (Grand Rapids, MI: Eerdmans, 2012).

15. Karl Rahner, *Theological Investigations*, vol. 5 (London: Darton, Longman & Todd, 1966), 121, 125.

16. Paul Knitter, *Introducing Theologies of Religions* (Maryknoll, NY: Orbis Books, 2002), 77.

17. Ibid.

of all argue that it is simply impossible to judge the salvific potential of another religion. One need not go as far as a cultural-linguistic perspective to recognize that one can only speak experientially from and about one's own religious life and tradition. Hence, all one can "know" as a Christian is that the ritual and spiritual life of Christianity lead to the experience of salvation. From within a Christian faith perspective, one can neither confidently affirm nor deny the possibility of attaining salvation through other religions.

There has been much discussion on the unity or diversity of religious experiences and on the question of whether all religions lead to the same ultimate religious end. While perennial philosophers such as Aldous Huxley[18] and Frithjof Schuon[19] and pluralist theologians such as John Hick[20] have argued that all religions are based on the same fundamental religious experience and oriented to the same ultimate reality, constructivist philosophers of mysticism such as Stephen Katz[21] and inclusivist theologians such as Mark Heim have emphasized the essential relationship between language and experience or between practice and goal, thus emphasizing the distinctiveness of religious experiences and ultimate ends. Those arguing for the oneness of all religious ends tend to regard all particular religious ends as various expressions of the same ultimate reality and goal. They focus mainly on mystical texts and on the fruits of mystical experiences to support this position.[22] In his book *Salvations*, Mark Heim counters this argument by focusing on the essential relationship between means and end, or religious practice and ultimate goal. Seeking to preserve "the maximum truth value in the specifics of the traditions"[23] he points

---

18. Aldous Huxley, *The Perennial Philosophy* (New York: Harper & Brothers, 1945).

19. Frithjof Schuon, *The Transcendent Unity of Religions* (New York: Harper & Row, 1984).

20. John Hick, *God Has Many Names* (London: Macmillan, 1980).

21. Steven Katz, ed., *Mysticism and Philosophical Analysis* (New York: Oxford University Press, 1978).

22. William James's *The Varieties of Religious Experience* (1907) was a particularly influential text for all of these thinkers.

23. Mark Heim, *Salvations: Truth and Difference in Religion* (Maryknoll, NY: Orbis Books, 1999), 145.

out that Jewish religious practice is not oriented toward the Christian understanding of salvation, and the pursuit of *moksha* or nirvana in Hinduism or Buddhism cannot be simply identified with the desire for salvation in Christianity. Without going into further details of the debate, it is safe to say that the question of the unity or diversity of religious experiences and ends cannot be resolved in purely phenomenological terms. Since ultimate religious experiences are essentially ineffable and the final religious goal by definition eschatological, there is no neutral or historical place from which to compare them.

While the debate is thus phenomenologically unresolvable, it is natural for religions to seek to assess the value of other religions in terms of their own specific goal. Even Mark Heim developed a theology in which the ends of other religions came to be regarded as penultimate with regard to the Christian religious end, and thus as ultimately oriented toward a Christian understanding of salvation.[24] However, the belief that all religions are ultimately oriented to one's own religious end, or that the religious ends of other religions are ultimately subsumed in one's own religious end skirts over the problem of conflicting truth claims or incompatible teachings and practices in other religions. It would be incoherent to state that other religions are entirely or equally ways to salvation when they at times contain teachings and practices opposed to Christianity. And even when teachings and practices appear to be similar to those of Christianity, the broader religious context in which they are embedded often imbues them with meanings that are not always compatible with Christian teachings. As such, even O'Collins, in interpreting the Vatican documents as suggesting that other religions do offer ways to salvation, qualifies this by stating that "this is not the same thing as (a) alleging that they are equally effective at putting people in contact with God, or (b) acknowledging them to be complete and clear ways, equivalent to what God offers through Jesus Christ and the community called into being by the Holy Spirit."[25] Hence, from a Christian theological perspective, one cannot unequivocally designate other religions, or even aspects of

---

24. Mark Heim, *The Depth of the Riches: A Trinitarian Theology of Religious Ends* (Grand Rapids, MI: Eerdmans, 2001).

25. O'Collins, *The Second Vatican Council*, 163.

other religions, as ways to salvation. But neither can one simply deny them salvific efficacy. The Bible clearly affirms the universal salvific will of God (1 Tim 2:4), and Karl Rahner's argument about the necessary social and historical nature of salvation[26] cannot be easily refuted. Moreover, while religious teachings are indeed colored by their overall religious context, they often do contain a certain number of moral and religious teachings that are plainly similar or the same as Christianity. To deny any salvific efficacy to other religions would then also be incoherent. Rather than affirming or denying other religions as ways to salvation, it is thus logically and theologically sound to maintain an attitude of humble ignorance on the question.

The virtue of refraining from judging the salvific potential of other religions in general is not only an expression of humility but also of prudence. The world of religious diversity is immense, and it would be impossible to make blanket statements about all religions. The religions mentioned in the Vatican II documents (Hinduism, Buddhism, Islam, Judaism) represent only a fraction of the existing religions in the world. While these religions have certainly survived the test of time, each contains significant internal diversity and conflict, thus precluding general judgments of these religions as a whole. In addition, there are thousands of old and new religions in the world which cannot be a priori judged ways of salvation, or not. As such, an attitude of agnosticism regarding the salvific value of other religions appears to be existentially, phenomenologically, and theologically coherent, without diminishing the possibility and the importance of dialogue with other religions.

Soteriological Agnosticism and Interreligious Dialogue

In keeping the middle between affirming other religions as means of salvation and denying them any salvific power, the documents of Vatican II allow for genuine exploration of the truth of other religions and mutual learning. While the texts do not pass judgment on the salvific

---

26. Rahner states, "If . . . man can always have a positive, saving relationship to God, and if he always had to have it, then he always had to have it within *that* religion which in practice was at his disposal by being a factor in his sphere of existence." See *Theological Investigations*, vol. 5, 126.

power of religions as a whole, they do explicitly affirm the presence of elements of truth and holiness in other religions. *Nostra aetate* 2 states unambiguously that

> The Catholic Church rejects nothing that is true and holy in these religions. She regards with sincere reverence those ways of conduct and of life, those precepts and teachings which, though differing in many aspects from the ones she holds and sets forth, nonetheless often reflect a ray of that Truth which enlightens all people.

It is important to emphasize that this text forms the first official recognition by the church of the presence of truth in other religions. The text goes on to state that

> The Church, therefore, exhorts her sons and daughters, that through dialogue and collaboration with the followers of other religions, carried out with prudence and love and in witness to the Christian faith and life, they recognize, preserve and promote the good things, spiritual and moral, as well as the sociocultural values found among these peoples.

Among the conditions for the possibility of dialogue with other religions, recognition of the (possible) presence of truth in the other religion constitutes both a necessary and a sufficient condition.[27] For a religion oriented toward the eschatological fulfillment of the truth and based on the belief in the continuing revelation of truth in history, the very possibility that this truth might reveal itself in other religions ought to propel it to discovering that truth and engaging it in a constructive way. Rather than on the salvific status of other religions, theology of religions might thus focus more explicitly on the epistemological questions regarding the nature and status of truth in other religions, its relationship to Christian truth claims, and the process of discerning such truth. Such a shift from soteriological to epistemological questions may also put to rest the ongoing debate over the relationship between theology of religions and comparative theology.

---

27. For a more in-depth discussion of the conditions for dialogue see my *The Im-Possibility of Interreligious Dialogue* (New York: Crossroad, 2008).

Weary of the endless internal Christian debate over the salvific status of other religions, comparative theologians such as Jim Fredericks and Francis Clooney have argued for the importance of simply engaging the other religion and then possibly determining its truth and value.[28] They thus reject the idea that comparative theology requires a theology of religions. However, if theology of religions focuses on the question of truth rather than salvation, it becomes more evident that any engagement with other religions involves at least some presupposition about the possibility of finding truth in the other religion. Granted, the question whether there actually is truth in another religion and how that truth relates to Christian teachings can only be determined after in fact engaging that tradition. But the two disciplines may then be regarded mutually informing in a constructive way. In bracketing the question of salvation from theology of religions, the simple and inevitable epistemic function of theology of religions thus becomes more evident.

One of the critiques of the Vatican II approach to dialogue is its somewhat paternalizing and domesticating attitude to the truth of other religions. While encouraging Christians to enter into "discussion and collaboration" with members of other religions, the text speaks mainly of acknowledging, preserving, and encouraging the truths found in other religions. It does not also speak of *learning from* other religions. However, there are significant resources within the Vatican II documents that point to the possibility of a mutually enriching dialogue. First, when referring to other religions, *Nostra aetate* speaks of precepts and doctrines that *"although differing in many ways from her own teaching,* nevertheless often reflect a ray of that truth which enlightens all men." This (often missed) clause suggests that other religions may reveal elements of truth that are significantly different from those that the church already holds, and from which she may thus learn.

Second, insofar as the possibility of learning from other religions requires a certain degree of humility about one's own understand-

---

28. The most systematic argument for this position may be found in James Fredericks, *Faith among Faiths: Christian Theology and Non-Christian Religions* (Mahwah, NJ: Paulist Press, 1999).

ing of the truth, the Vatican document *Dei verbum* 8 states that "the Church is always advancing toward the plenitude of divine truth, until eventually the words of God are fulfilled in her." This eschatological understanding of the truth thus allows for the possibility of growth, including through dialogue with other religions. It is thus not surprising that later Vatican documents, such as *Dialogue and Proclamation* (1990), become more explicit about the possibility of learning from other religions:

> The fullness of truth received in Jesus Christ does not give individual Christians the guarantee that they have grasped that truth fully. In the last analysis truth is not a thing we possess but a person by whom we must allow ourselves to be possessed. This is an unending process. While keeping their identity intact, Christians must be prepared to learn and to receive from and through others the positive value of their tradition. (49)

Since Vatican II, Catholics have indeed been actively engaged in all types of interreligious dialogue, from the summoning of religious leaders to pray for peace (in Assisi) to the official founding of a monastic interreligious dialogue (DIM/MID), and from various forms of grassroots initiatives to the development of new theological disciplines devoted to dialogue with particular religions (comparative theology). All of this has been possible without a clear and definitive pronouncement on the salvific status of other religions.

Conclusion

While some have lamented the reticence of Vatican II in taking a position on the salvific value of other religions, I believe that this reserve reflects a theological and a practical wisdom that is still to be fully appreciated and explored. To pronounce other religions as ways of salvation would have contradicted the self-understanding of those religions while also overstepping the boundaries of what one might claim to know theologically. The church unambiguously affirms the possibility of salvation outside the church. But what the particular role is of the religions in this process of salvation would be impossible to assess from within the theological purview of a particular religion. One may hope and even expect that God uses the religions to lead their respective followers to the ultimate and eternal goal. But to make a blanket statement about this would be both presumptuous and unnecessary for genuine dialogue to take place.

A shift away from the question of the salvific nature of non-Christian religions to their potential for revealing divine truth might moreover set a clearer and more crisp agenda for the discipline of theology of religions and establish its proper, and necessary, place in relation to comparative theology.

Future Directions
for the Church

9

Set into the Future
The Role of the Laity

PAUL LAKELAND

Ten years ago I wrote a book about the fortunes of the laity in today's Roman Catholic Church. Entitled *The Liberation of the Laity: In Search of an Accountable Church*, it traced the failure of church leadership over the previous forty years to implement the vision of lay apostolicity professed in the documents of Vatican II and sought an end to the continuing infantilization of laypeople. As recently as two years ago I would have had no reason to revise any of the judgments I made in that book. Today, thanks to the advent of Pope Francis, there are good reasons for renewed hope that the time of waiting is passing and that we can now reasonably return to the future proposed at Vatican II. Following upon a string of remarks he made here and there on the appropriate role of laypeople, Pope Francis addressed the issue more formally in section 102 of his November 2013 Apostolic Exhortation, *Evangelii gaudium*. "Lay people," he writes, "are, put simply, the vast majority of the people of God," while "the minority—ordained ministers—are at their service." While the understanding of the role of laypeople has been growing in the church, he says, "a clear awareness of this responsibility of the laity, grounded in their baptism and confirmation, does not appear in the same way in all places." Sometimes this is caused by the failure to educate laypeople to take on more responsibility, sometimes "because in their particular Churches room has not been made for them to speak and to act, due to an excessive clericalism which keeps them away from decision-making." Repeating remarks that he had made quite frequently in the first six months of his papacy, the pope added that while there are many more people involved in lay ministries, "this involvement is not reflected in a greater penetration of Christian values in the social, political and economic sectors." "It often remains tied to tasks within the church," he concludes, "without a real commitment to applying the Gospel to the transformation of society."[1]

This single paragraph in the papal document reprises the major points of conciliar teaching on the laity. First, in reminding the church of the relationship between lay and ordained Pope Francis recalls the preferred ecclesial image of "the people of God." Second, he anchors the responsibilities of the laity in their baptism and confirmation, returning to Vatican II's concern to foreground the baptismal priesthood. Third, in his concern to stress the apostolic role of the laity in evangelizing the world he echoes, if he does not explicitly refer to, the conciliar definition of the laity as "essentially secular," an idea as important as it has been misunderstood. Fourth, he indicates the need for collaboration between clergy and laity in charting a future course. And finally, he warns against resistance to the vision of Vatican II occasioned by "clericalism." For Francis, clericalism is the sin of "self-referentiality" in which all sectors of the church, lay and ordained alike, are tempted to rest in a comfortably centripetal mindset, forgetting that the gospel is there to be spread. As he said in a homily less than a month after his election, if we recognize our apostolic responsibilities to the world, "the Church becomes a mother Church that produces children," but if we descend into self-referentiality "the Church is not the mother, but the babysitter, that takes care of the baby—to put the baby to sleep." It becomes "a Church dormant." So, he concludes, "let us reflect on our baptism, on the responsibility of our baptism."[2]

In what follows I propose to explore in a little more depth this set of issues, beginning from the rediscovery of baptism and the notion of the baptismal priesthood and moving on to a consideration of lay apostolicity. While this will entail at least a brief reminder of the central elements of conciliar teaching, the thrust here is toward the future. Given the clear teaching of the Council, which is central to the papal

---

1. Not the least of the changes since Pope Francis was elected is the much more user-friendly format used to present this document.

2. Homily at Casa Sancta Marthae, April 17, 2013.

platform for change in the church, how do we move into the future? What needs to happen to make the conciliar vision live? What needs to change and what can remain the same? To frame the question in terms of a remark that Yves Congar made toward the end of his long life, what will it mean to live in a church in which "it is no longer the layman who stands in need of definition, but the priest"?[3] As Pope Francis's remarks above make evident, one cannot explain the church in terms of the 2 percent (at most) who are ordained to serve the 98 percent. One must rather explore the meaning of the 2 percent relative to the whole body of the faithful; and once one places the stress upon evangelization—however broadly conceived—the laity come to the fore. In a self-referential church the vast lay majority turn to the clergy for the sacraments as means to an ecclesial spirituality oriented to "my" salvation. In a more apostolic church salvation is connected to my participation in the work of spreading the gospel more than in my conformity to the rules and regulations of a cozy and even self-congratulatory community.

Let us begin then with baptism. The primary structural feature for understanding the nature of the church's apostolic activity and in particular that of the laity is baptism, but for at least a thousand years our church has been suffering from what I can only call baptismal amnesia. We simply forgot about baptism, or, more correctly, we overlooked any significance to baptism beyond its status as a sacrament of initiation. When the church came to be thought of simply as the place where salvation is possible, perhaps even the only place, then baptism was entry into the community of the saved, and obedient life within that community was the ticket to salvation. But once the focus shifted back to a notion of the church as the place from which the message of salvation is proclaimed to the world beyond it, baptism as entry into the church had to be seen as a call to mission. In baptism the new Christian is commissioned to proclaim the good news that "God so loved the world that he sent his only-begotten Son" (John 3:16). While there is a lot of room to talk about how the good news is to be proclaimed and reason to place more stress in some contexts

---

3. Yves Congar, "My Pathfindings in the Theology of Laity and Ministries," *The Jurist* 2 (1972): 181-82.

on the love of God and less on the gift of the Son, there is absolutely
no question that proclamation of the good news is the mission of the
church. It is through participation in this mission that salvation comes
to the baptized.

The commissioning that occurs in baptism (and confirmation, the
completion of the sacrament that was separated off when infant baptism became the norm) confers baptismal priesthood or "the priesthood of all the faithful" upon the baptized. Essentially, then, "priesthood" is simply a term to describe the Christian life. The community
of the baptized *is* the priestly community. Baptism and priesthood are
in this sense tautologous. As priestly people we represent God to the
world and bring the concerns of the world before God, sharing somehow in the one priesthood of Christ that is so clearly laid out in the
Letter to the Hebrews and reprised at length in *Lumen gentium*. The
ordained or ministerial priesthood has to be understood in relation
to the baptismal priesthood, which it exists to serve. Pope Francis's
comment to this effect, quoted above, echoes the well-known remark
of John Henry Newman that without the laity, the clergy would "look
strange." Their primary role, in consequence of this insight, is not that
of offering sacrifice, not even the sacrifice of the Mass, but of servant
leadership of the apostolic community of faith. The ordained minister
presides at the Eucharist because he is called to be the servant leader
of those, the laity, whose task it is to sanctify the world.

The distinct roles and separation of function between the baptismal
and ministerial priesthood are indicated in the important though curiously illogical statement in *Lumen gentium* that the two priesthoods
"differ in essence and not only in degree."[4] Difference in essence is
hugely important, because it makes it impossible to imagine baptismal
priesthood as somehow lesser than ordained priesthood. The baptized
layperson is not less priestly than the ordained; it is simply that he or
she has not added to the baptismal priesthood the particular responsibilities of servant leadership that denote the role of the ordained.
This also shows, if such a demonstration were necessary, that ordination is not a passing from a lower or lesser to a fuller or higher form
of priesthood, but the addition of a second priesthood to a baptismal

---

4. *Lumen gentium* 10.

priesthood that the ordained continue to possess. The Council's addition of the phrase "not only in degree" to the assertion of the essential difference between the two priesthoods is of course a logistical solecism of which they should not be proud. One cannot have two things that are essentially different and at the same time different in degree. The two priesthoods either differ in essence or in degree. They cannot do both.[5] The church for many centuries before Vatican II, if it considered baptismal priesthood at all, would have considered it a lesser priesthood than the higher calling of ordination. After Vatican II this is no longer an option.

The implications for the future of the church of this understanding of the two priesthoods and the relationship between them are incalculable. While they do not overturn the mission of ordained ministry as a calling to servant leadership, they clearly envisage a shift of energy in the church. Once we think of the church as an apostolic community of faith then the work of the whole people, 98 percent of whom are laity, needs to be the center of attention. If the church had a strategic plan—and who is to say that it shouldn't?—it would be ordered to answering the question, How can the laity be better energized to exercise their essentially apostolic role? And as the answer to that question is considered, debated, and eventually determined, it will surely lead to changing the structures of church life. Since at the present day most Catholic Christians would not understand if they were told of their baptismal priesthood and would not see themselves as called to apostolic ministry, since most Catholic Christians in today's church consider their membership of the church to be exhausted by liturgical celebration and the ethical life, it is evident that the structures of the church creak, to say the least. What the church is *for* has to dictate *how* the church is. But at the present, how the church is tends on the whole to impede the clarity of its mission to be the voice of the good news in the world. So what are we going to do about it?

Any changes in the church that are going to last must be anchored

---

5. It seems likely that the addition of the phrase "not only in degree" was a sop to more traditional elements among the Council fathers who were reluctant to countenance any less hierarchical understanding of the respective importance of the two priesthoods.

in the life of the local community as much if not more than in the words of the pope or bishops. What leadership can do more effectively than the individual Christian or local community is stimulate the necessary process of reflection. When Pope Francis proclaims that the church needs to place the concerns of the world's poor in the foreground of its sense of self it is easy and even expedient to give notional assent. But real assent occurs only when the community of faith internalizes conversion to the poor and changes its pastoral practice accordingly. What will make such real assent possible, once the mind of the pope has been made clear? There seem to be at least three important steps. First, the reeducation of all the church to the meaning of the two priesthoods and the understanding of the process of discernment, decision, and leadership that follows. Second, a renewed familiarity with the Scriptures, one that will show the extent to which the biblical God is especially concerned for the poor and vulnerable. And third, the development of a more sophisticated social awareness on the part of Christians that will lead to confidently living out the order of values proclaimed in the gospel. These three steps are not placed here in chronological order or in order of importance; on the contrary, we need to begin on all three at once, if the church is to have a worthwhile future.

Priesthood and Leadership

Once we "get" the message of Vatican II on the nature and relationship of the two priesthoods it is not difficult to see that there need to be major changes in the way parish life is conducted. In the first place, the ordained minister needs to be understood to be leading the community from within, not from above. If his ordination had led to the abandonment of the baptismal priesthood, if ordained ministry were to be understood as a higher or more complete priesthood than baptismal priesthood, then one might consider the ordained minister to be leading from above the body of the faithful. However, as one of the faithful and one of the members of the baptismal priesthood, leading from within is the only option. Of course, this does not mean that the minister is no longer the leader, only that leadership needs to be rethought, in fact along the lines of effective leadership in society as a whole, and not on the pattern of military leadership.[6] Effective leadership in business, in education, and even in politics has much more to do with enabling the gifts of others than it does with telling them what to do. And while many fine pastors know this and already do exactly this, neither the canonical structures of the church nor the practice and self-understanding of the episcopate seems to support it. When a pastor allows final decision making to a parochial pastoral council, composed largely of laypeople, he is in contravention of canon law. When a minister cedes the pulpit to an unordained person, he is in serious danger of sanction by the bishop. When he separates himself entirely from all parish finances and leaves them in the hands of a lay committee, he not only makes a personally healthy step for himself, he also in most situations runs counter to the diocesan understanding of the parish corporation.

As we look to the future of the parish, we need in the first place to educate the community to see that the one who presides at the Eucharist does so for and on behalf of the community whose Eucharist it is, and does so *because* he is the servant leader of this local community. The ordained priest is not the leader because he says the Mass; he says the Mass because he is the leader. Ordination is not hieratic promotion but the church's recognition that the one ordained is called and qualified to serve as servant leader. Second, we need to change our whole approach to seminary education in order to reflect a better understanding of what it is the candidate for ordination is being called to. And third, we have to change parish life to make this changed understanding real.

Today's lay Catholics are adult in a way that two or three generations ago may not have been the case. They are better educated than previous generations, sometimes even better educated in theology and the history of religion than their pastors, and along with this higher education goes more confidence about their roles in the church. No one who is a competent professional finds it easy to step into a "sheep and shepherd" model of church life. After Vatican II, no one should have to. This has to mean, among other things, that decisions about

---

6. Though even in the military it is important to gain the confidence of those who serve under you.

the local parish are made by the community or their elected representatives, not by the pastor alone. It also has to mean that financial responsibility for the parish has to be in the hands of elected representatives of those who supply the funds, namely, the laity. If this means changing the structure of the parish corporation, so be it (and sometimes, as in my home state of Connecticut, this cannot be done without changing state law). And it should lead to appropriate oversight and evaluation procedures that check on the work of the elected bodies and that provide the pastor and other responsible persons with regular feedback about their job performance.

The Word of God in Scripture

More important than these healthy managerial steps, however, is the new orientation to pastoral priorities that can and should follow. Here is where the pastor's light hand on the tiller may have to become a little heavier, since the gospel leaves us no choice but to prefer the poor, while human nature tends to make us more attuned to our own good. And here is where a renewed attention to Scripture is essential. Most well-functioning parishes have Bible study groups, but few have an ongoing biblical catechesis that ties the work of the parish to the priorities of the gospel.

When we turn to educating ourselves on the gospel preference for the poor and vulnerable, we are inevitably led to the biblical exegesis of liberation theology. Fortunately for us today we have a pope who is neither afraid of the priorities of liberation theology nor unable to distinguish between its wisdom and the categories of Marxist analysis which some of its proponents have employed. It was not irrelevant that one of Pope Francis's earliest meetings was with Gustavo Gutiérrez, the father of liberation theology. Their mutual affection and obvious affinity was based not on their common use of Marxist categories but because each sees in the other a person whose life has been devoted to the poor. Notably, the base Christian communities of liberation theology have been primarily the work of poor Christians, supplying in their own local communities for the absence of traditional parochial structures, and using their gatherings to reflect on the relationship between the word of God in Scripture and the necessary initiatives for the promotion of dignified human life in a context of poverty and oppression. Their energies and courage over many years now stem from the awareness that the God of the Bible actively sides with the poor. To the poor, the Word is a blessing; to the rest of us, it can be a challenge or a condemnation. The choice is ours.

It may be that the poor of the global South, especially in Latin America, have shown those of us in the affluent North the way out of our growing ecclesial predicament. Like them, to a much lesser degree thus far, we suffer from a shortage of ordained ministers. The base Christian community is an initiative of lay leadership under the protection of the local bishop through which reflection on Scripture leads naturally to actions to improve the religious and social climate in which the community exists. In Latin America it was also in large part a movement to develop the self-confidence of the laity in leading worship and in promoting social action. Most notably, the majority of so-called "delegates of the word," officially appointed leaders, were and are women. So, while the economic and educational level of North American Catholic laity might be quite different from that of our brothers and sisters to the south, we have much to learn from them about how to conduct ecclesial life in the context of diminishing traditional resources.

Becoming a Prophetic Community

When the local community of faith turns from its new awareness of the message of God in the Bible to the question of what precise pastoral priorities should follow, the final building block that it needs is a sophisticated and critical understanding of social issues, local, national, and global. Without such awareness the pastoral initiatives of the community may do much good, but will lack a coherent focus. It is one thing to care for the poor, another to address the causes of poverty. The first without the second is endless, while the second without the first is a dry abstraction. Together, they show the head and the heart united in discipleship with Christ, who fed the hungry and bound up the wounds of the victims, but who also lived to proclaim the coming of the Reign of God in which a new order of values would prevail and the lion would lie down with the lamb.

To achieve the kind of sociopolitical awareness that will make the countercultural impact of global Catholicism as effective as it can and should be we need another layer of catechesis, one that may very well be the primary responsibility of the baptismal priesthood rather than the ordained. This catechesis needs to be directed toward the compassionate defense of life in a complex and pluralistic world, and should not be confused with simplistic directives to "solve" difficult ethical dilemmas. There is lots of evidence that the church of the global north is failing to find a focal point from which to proclaim the relevance of the gospel to the problems of today's world. Generally speaking the episcopate wishes to promote a fairly hard line on matters of personal and sexual ethics but is willing to recognize legitimate difference of opinion on most if not all issues of social ethics (while Pope Francis seems to take the opposite position). Laypeople, on the other hand, seem on the whole to be more tolerant of variations in approaches to questions of personal and sexual ethics, while quite divided among themselves on matters of social and political morality. Taking the United States as an example, perhaps a more coherent ethical framework on the part of the teaching church would make it less likely that the range of Catholic views on, say, the death penalty or immigration would match fairly closely those of Americans as a whole.

The "Essential Secularity" of the Baptismal Priesthood

When *Lumen gentium* taught the essential secularity of the lay state, it proclaimed a truth at once profound and misleading. The challenge of interpreting this statement, of course, is the meaning of the word "secular." In much contemporary religious discourse "the secular" is the world empty of God and often understood to be antagonistic toward religion. At the very least, it means the world in the sense of the worldly. If we begin here, then to declare the laity to be "essentially secular" would be to suggest that fundamentally they are worldly people, presumably to be organized, corrected, or even "saved" by the ordained ministers whose job it is to proclaim sacred as opposed to secular values and remind the laity of "what is really important," namely, a religious vision that draws us out of this world.

Vatican II in no way wished to suggest that the "essential secularity" of the laity meant that they needed rescuing, nor indeed that the world in which they live out their lives was essentially opposed to religion. To be sure we get the picture right, we need to recall our earlier consideration of the baptismal priesthood. To be a Christian is to be priestly, we saw, and to be priestly is to somehow mediate the things of God to the world and to bring the hopes and fears of the world before God in worship and prayer. The relationship, then, between the baptismal priesthood and the world in which it is exercised is very much that expressed in the image of "the leaven in the mass." Flour is good, but it will not become bread without interaction with yeast. Yeast is not better than flour, nor is flour better than yeast. But both must collaborate in the making of bread. Yeast without flour is nasty, while flour without yeast is inert. Moreover, yeast can become tired and old, and then it does not do the job for which it was intended. So to be essentially secular is simply to be a Christian in the world, even perhaps a worldly Christian, and so—and with no addition—an apostle. God, one might say, chooses neither flour nor yeast, but instead wills the making of bread, the fruitful interaction between the members of the baptismal priesthood and the great mass of humanity whom God loves and calls, each in her or his own way.

If indeed the essential secularity of the laity is a way of asserting the proper context of their apostolic activity, yet this characteristic of "essential secularity" does demand one caveat. If we call the laity essentially secular and see the context of their apostolicity to be the secular world, then we have to be careful not to allow this clear separation of function between the laity and the ordained to imply a rigid distinction, still less a hierarchy of the more and the less important. Once again, we might employ the image of yeast and flour, albeit more loosely and with less direct connection to the gospel usage. *Functionally*, the ordained are the yeast and the laity are the flour in the division of labor in the church. The ordained sustain and animate, through their preaching and the administration of the sacraments, the apostolic activity of the whole community. However, *essentially* the ordained and the laity are always already truly bread, because they all share the baptismal priesthood. Once again, it is hard not to see ordination as functional rather than hieratic, and to a degree *Lumen gentium* supports this in its reminder that the ordained are also sometimes involved in the things of this world—just as the laity are sometimes called to serve particular roles within the church, roles that might in a previous age have been exercised by the ordained or those in religious life.

Looking to the Future

It remains to raise a few questions arising from the picture we have drawn here of the apostolicity of the laity and the right relationship between the laity and the ordained on the one hand, and the church and the world on the other. Before doing so, it is important to recall the earlier remarks about the local community of faith as the primary locus for building the future of the church. When "the church" is featured in the press or other media, it is invariably the ordained leadership of the community of faith, national or global, that is under scrutiny. But when we ask where the church *really* is, the answer has to be wherever the community of faith is gathered in prayer and worship as a source and fount of divine grace, not in the halls of ecclesiastical bureaucracy or the diocesan offices. They are at best enablers of the work of the gospel, at worst a hindrance and even occasions of scandal.

The first question has to do with the division of labor between the ordained and the laity. If the role of the ordained is to nurture and sustain the lay vanguard in its apostolic activity in the world, then ought we not to reconceive the role of the ordained as those who spend their lives doing precisely this? Leadership of the local community is the fundamental responsibility of the ordained, which would suggest that those who are the leaders of the local community should be those who are ordained to serve it. So, as we move away from the essentially magical medieval understanding of priesthood as the acquisition of extraordinary powers we will be forced to ask again just who should be ordained, and who is disqualified and why if indeed their calling is to work within the community of faith to strengthen it for apostolic activity, rather than—as is the lay calling—to be fundamentally oriented to apostolic activity in the world.

A second question must be asked, this time about the role of authority relative to apostolic activity. First, as individuals, members of the baptismal priesthood exercise their ministry in the world under the authority of their baptism and require no commissioning or approval by church authority. This is what it means simply to live one's life in the world as a believing Christian, giving witness to the gospel. Traditionally the church has argued that whenever an organization is formed in order to further the causes of the church it must have ecclesiastical approval if it wishes to claim the name Catholic. But when we think of the church's life, as we have here, as oriented constantly and comprehensively toward the proclamation of the good news, the situation changes. If the work of the church is in the secular world and the laity are essentially secular, then shouldn't it be the case that at least some of the authority for the scope and shape of the church's pastoral vision be in the hands of the experts? Pope Francis seems to recognize this in comments on the role of the bishop relative to the people. Sometimes, he says, the bishop must lead, and sometimes he must be one among the whole body of the faithful. But sometimes, he continues, the bishop must stand aside because often the laity "have the scent of the way." I take this to mean that the wisdom of the lay faithful needs to be allowed to flourish and that a wise bishop knows when to step aside. Moreover, these words are from our current pope, for whom the church is fundamentally apostolic and her besetting sin is self-referentiality. Might we then look to a future in which lay authority and lay leadership in the apostolic mission of the church will be given a much bigger role than it currently has. And how shall that happen? Perhaps the pope will include lay leaders in future episcopal synods. Perhaps, though I think it unlikely, he will appoint lay cardinals. Or perhaps he will act on his evident wish for devolution to promote the role of the diocesan synod, which canon law requires to have a substantial lay representation. Canon law leaves it to the local bishop to determine when a synod should be called. Pope Francis's new broom ought to be hinting strongly to bishops around the world that now might be the time to blow the dust off this important but much neglected channel of communication.

A third and final question brings us back to the preferential option for the poor so strongly stated by our present pope. Globally, it is easy to see what needs to be done if not always so easy to have the strength of will to make it happen. Proclaiming the gospel in the world, the work of the laity, *has* to mean taking any and every opportunity to promote a different order of priorities from those currently employed in global capitalism and the self-centered myopia of the wealthy nations. There are many lay Catholics in important positions in political life around the world, perhaps especially so in the U.S. House and Senate. How depressing that so few of them seem to recognize the demands of global justice and are willing to put the public good ahead of their own political fortunes. But the more immediate challenge for most of us is to make the preferential option for the poor in our own backyard. Fundamentally this is not about handouts or "helping the poor." It is much more a matter of allowing the voice and needs of the poor to dictate our parochial, local, and regional agendas. Here again we face the sin of self-referentiality. It may be that in the last analysis a viable future for our church requires us to throw aside this preoccupation with ourselves. The laity can begin this process by rejecting an inward-looking, clericalized church in favor of one that reaches out to succor the hopes and fears of the world, especially those of the poor and oppressed.

10

Novus habitus mentis
A New Way of Thinking
about Ordained Ministry

W hat a year this has been for anyone interested in the life of the Catholic Church. While celebrations continued marking the fiftieth anniversaries of various highlights of the Second Vatican Council (1962-1965), two other events took place with their own proper historic significance. First, Pope Benedict XVI stunned the world when he courageously resigned from the papal office, citing the vicissitudes of age. Of all the things Joseph Ratzinger has done in service to the church over his lifetime, none will carry the import of this act of humble service. Paired with the papal resignation, of course, was the conclave and election of the first pope from the Americas, Jorge Mario Bergoglio, the retired archbishop of Buenos Aires. On a seemingly daily basis from the day of his election, the new pope has been stunning the world. Becoming the first pope to take the name of Francis, he has become known for his surprising and refreshing approach to the Petrine ministry. Pope Francis has come to exemplify many things to many people, who recognize in him a new style of leadership, a new way of approaching life and ministry. A retired bishop remarked recently, "I never thought I would be this excited again about what happens in Rome!" To understand what is happening, we turn the clock back to October 11, 1962.

During his address opening the Second Vatican Council, Pope John XXIII spoke of the balance between the "sacred deposit of Christian doctrine" and its relationship to the changing demands of the contemporary world.

In order, however, that this doctrine may influence the numerous fields of human activity, with reference to individuals, to families, and to social life, it is necessary first of all that the Church should never depart from the sacred patrimony of truth received from the Fathers. But at the same time she must ever look to the present, to the new conditions and new forms of life introduced into the modern world, which have opened new avenues to the Catholic apostolate.... The substance of the ancient doctrine of the deposit of faith is one thing, and the way in which it is presented is another.[1]

And there is the challenge. How do we balance those things that cannot change with those that can? Four years later the bishops of the Council provided some additional detail in *Gaudium et spes* 4:

To carry out such a task, the Church has always had the duty of scrutinizing the signs of the times and of interpreting them in the light of the Gospel. Thus, in language intelligible to each generation, she can respond to the perennial questions which people ask about this present life and the life to come, and about the relationship of the one to the other. We must therefore recognize and understand the world in which we live, its explanations, its longings, and its often dramatic characteristics.

After the Council ended in 1965, Pope Paul VI began speaking of a *novus habitus mentis* to describe the way the revised Code of Canon Law would need to be approached, in light of the ecclesiologies of the Second Vatican Council. Just as the 1917 Code reflected the vision of church from Vatican I (1869-1870), the "new" Code would have to mirror, enable, and empower the church as described by Vatican II. "Now, however, with changing conditions ... canon law must be prudently reformed; specifically, it must be accommodated to a new way of thinking proper to the second ecumenical Council of the Vatican, in which pastoral care and new needs of the people of God are met."[2]

---

1. John XXIII, "Allocution for the Opening of the Second Vatican Council," *Acta apostolicae sedis*, v. LIV (1962): 786-96 n. 14.

2. Paul VI, address to the cardinals and the consultants of the Council for the Code Revision of Canon Law, November 20, 1965, *Acta apostolicae sedis*, v. LVII (1965), 998.

All of this was echoed by John Paul II in the Apostolic Constitution *Sacrae disciplinae leges*, promulgating the 1983 Code of Canon Law, when he wrote:

This new Code could be understood as a great effort to translate this same doctrine, that is, the conciliar ecclesiology, into canonical language. If, however, it is impossible to translate perfectly into canonical language the conciliar image of the Church, nevertheless, in this image there should always be found as far as possible its essential point of reference.[3]

This brings us back to the Council. As we saw above, Pope Paul observed that the "new way of thinking" is not properly directed simply at the revision of canon law itself; rather, the revision is to reflect the prior "new way of thinking" already experienced by, through, and in the Council. We must then look closer at this "new way of thinking" proper to the second ecumenical Council of the Vatican."

Distinguished canonist Ladislas Örsy wrote about this term that "to acquire a new disposition of the mind means to enter into a new field of vision; that is, into a new horizon."[4] While this is not the place for an extended analysis of the terms involved, or even for a comprehensive review of the literature on the subject, at least a brief reflection on the theological—as well as canonical[5]—richness of the expression is warranted.

Dominican theologian Aidan Nichols, in *The Shape of Catholic Theology*, introduces his readers to the activity of theology by referring to the "habit of theology." He then offers the famous insight of Yves Congar, who wrote, "theology is the highest of the habits of mind that a Christian man or woman can acquire." Nichols summarizes, "This theological habit of mind, like all aspects of Christian existence, is at one and the same time absolutely ordinary and natural, yet entirely

---

3. John Paul II, Apostolic Constitution *Sacrae disciplinae leges*, January 25, 1983.

4. Ladislas Örsy, "The Meaning of *Novus Habitus Mentis*: The Search for New Horizons," *The Jurist* 48 (1988): 431.

5. See, e.g., Donald E. Heintschel, "... A New Way of Thinking," *The Jurist* 44 (1984): 41-7, and the aforementioned article by Örsy. See also Ladislas Örsy, "*Novus Habitus Mentis*: New Attitude of Mind," *The Jurist* 45 (1985): 251-58.

extraordinary and supernatural. It is natural in that it draws on the human ability to study. It is supernatural in that its root and source is divinely given faith in the self-revealing God."[6]

This *habitus theologicus* is a disposition to think and act in certain ways. It is a learned recognition that certain actions, certain patterns of behavior, certain attitudes are more in keeping with the best of who we are called to be, and so we choose to do certain things and to avoid others. This is why Thomas Aquinas described virtue itself as a "habit." Habits, as Nichols points out, are based in nature and find both their source and their end in the supernatural. There are habits of thinking, of feeling, of willing, religious and moral habits: all of which collectively form a hermeneutical framework for pastoral action.

All of this is found in the call to a *novus habitus mentis*. More than a new "way" of thinking, it is a challenge to develop whole new "habits" of thinking, being, and acting. Developing and exercising new habits can lead to the kind of courageous new pastoral approaches such as those being modeled by Pope Francis. This is truly a creative disposition that finds its source and its end in our relationship with God, and not merely human wisdom. Developing a new *habitus* in ministry can help keep one focused on the future, not merely repeating approaches of the past. "This is the way we've always done things here" can give way to "This is how we can best apply the lessons we've learned in the past to meet the demands of the future, with mutual love, respect, courage, and commitment to the highest ideals of what it means to be a disciple of Christ in the world today."

And this is what we are seeing in Pope Francis and the world's reaction to him. The first pope to have been ordained to the presbyterate following the Council, his own formation was imbued with the *novus mentis habitus* of the Council. To understand this further, and to see where it might lead us in our further reflection on the ordained ministries of the church, we must take another look at the event of the Council itself. Just what was the source of this "new way of thinking proper to the second ecumenical Council of the Vatican"?

---

6. Aidan Nichols, *The Shape of Catholic Theology: An Introduction to Its Sources, Principles, and History* (Collegeville, MN: Liturgical Press, 1991), 13-14, citing Y. M.-J. Congar, "*Theologia est altissimus inter habitus intellectuales acquisitos hominis Christiani,*" *La foi et la théologie* (Paris, 1962), 192.

The Second Vatican Council: A Vision Born behind Bars

Many have researched comprehensively the history of the Second Vatican Council.[7] Our purpose here is much more focused. *Why* did Pope John inspire such a visionary approach to the Council in the first place? As one retired U.S. bishop who attended all four sessions of the Council remarked in an interview shortly before his death, "Some of us American bishops thought that we were just going to Rome to reenact the Catechism and then go home." However, once the world's bishops had assembled and began their work, the demands and pastoral needs of the contemporary world church would not permit a superficial response. Probably none of the bishops who participated in the magnificent opening celebration on October 11, 1962 was expecting what was to come over the next four years. Our question is not so much what happened at the Council, but why? In the space permitted here, let me focus on just two elements of a response to that question.

First, as is well known, Vatican II was the largest assembly of the world's bishops ever in the life of the church, with more than 2,600 bishops at the opening ceremonies. Not only is the number of bishops important; so too was their great cultural diversity. Thanks to the efforts of several preconciliar popes, more and more bishops were clergy native to their own countries, rather than missionary bishops from Europe. This true internationalization of the world's episcopate resulted in a Council that enjoyed a diversity of language, culture, and history never before assembled in the world itself, let alone in the church. While there was unity in creedal belief among the bishops, of course, how this faith was to be lived in the world demanded answers that were varied and culturally diverse: a one-size-fits-all response was not going to be possible, adequate, or even desirable. A pastoral response that might work in Rome would not necessarily work in Buenos Aires, Dar-es-Salaam, Tokyo, or Boise.

What did these world's bishops bring with them into St. Peter's on that bright October morning in 1962? Before answering that ques-

---

7. See, e.g., Giuseppe Alberigo and Joseph A. Komonchak, eds., *History of Vatican II*, 5 vols., (Maryknoll, NY: Orbis Books; Leuven, Belgium: Peeters, 1995-2006; John W. O'Malley, *What Happened at Vatican II?* (Cambridge. MA: Harvard University Press, 2010).

tion, consider the following scenario. Imagine that Pope Francis has decided to convoke another Council, but this time not only bishops will attend. You have been invited to participate, and you will have the opportunity, as did those bishops at Vatican II, to address the whole assembly and to suggest proposed topics for discussion and debate. What would you want to talk about at this new Council? How would you arrive at this decision?

It would be completely natural to reflect first on the events and experiences of your own life. What were the turning points in life, or those events that forever changed you in your own journey of discipleship and ministry. For example, those who have lived through wars, economic crises, political revolutions, and so on would easily cite these as defining moments in their personal and collective lives, events that would influence their worldview ever after. As you prepare for this hypothetical new Council, what experiences would influence your own vision of what that Council might decide?

Certainly, this was the question being asked by the world's bishops prior to Vatican II. None of them had ever participated in a general council of the church before: this was going to be a once-in-a-lifetime opportunity. Shortly after Pope John's announcement of his decision to call the Council, the world's bishops (along with the deans of schools of Catholic theology and the heads of men's religious congregations) were asked to submit their *vota* on what should be talked about at the Council. Almost nine thousand items were proposed in response, and the range of topics was truly extraordinary. Questions related to moral issues were included, along with concerns about the celebration of the various sacraments of the church, organizational issues, relationships with the Roman Curia, and on and on. Some proposals were completely at odds with others. For example, some bishops wanted to talk about restructuring the various rites and ordinations that made up the sacrament of Holy Orders. One hundred and one proposals, representing almost two hundred bishops from around the world, addressed the idea of a renewed permanent diaconate alone! Other bishops wished to make all of the minor orders (porter, lector, exorcist, and acolyte) and the major orders of subdiaconate and diaconate permanent, while others wanted to eliminate the minor orders and the subdiaconate altogether.

But there was something even deeper going on. As historians such as John O'Malley and others have pointed out, the historical and cultural influences on the bishops were many and varied. But one way to underscore this impact would be to continue our earlier reflection: what experiences did these bishops bring with them into the Council aula?

As the bishops processed into St. Peter's Basilica, the Second World War had been over for less than twenty years, and its effects were still raw and fresh. Perhaps the question we might ask ourselves is this: Where were each of those Council fathers twenty years before? Pope John XXIII, for example, as Archbishop Angelo Roncalli, had been serving as papal nuncio to Turkey twenty years before, serving a Catholic minority while also working to help Jews escape Nazi death camps. Cardinal Leon Joseph Suenens of Belgium had been the Vice Rector of the University of Leuven, actively resisting the Nazi occupation of his country. He was placed on a Nazi death list, only narrowly avoiding imprisonment and execution when the Allies liberated Belgium. A young Karol Wojtyla, auxiliary bishop of Krakow in 1962, had been a manual laborer and preparing for the priesthood in secret twenty years before. In his 2004 message for the World Day of Peace, as Pope John Paul II, he would recall that World War II was "an abyss of violence, destruction, and death unlike anything previously known."[8] Certainly the Second World War was something that almost all of the Council fathers would have experienced in one way or another as younger men, and it would be something that would certainly inform their pastoral visions and decisions.

And in a particular way, consider the impact of the war through the lens of the concentration camp. Between 1933 and 1945, there were more than three hundred concentration camps throughout Germany and German-occupied territories. The first of these was the Dachau concentration camp outside Munich, and the Dachau camp served as the infamous model for later camps. Nearly three thousand priests were incarcerated at Dachau alone, with fewer than half surviving the war. Initially, the clergy (of all faiths) were to be incarcerated in the general prison population, but eventually they were moved into their

---

8. John Paul II, *2004 Message of World Peace*, January 1, 2004, #5.

own barracks, informally dubbed as *der Priesterblock* by their guards. During discussions while incarcerated, especially later in the war, several prisoners raised a number of possibilities concerning the renewal of the church following the war. For example, Fr. Wilhelm Schamoni, S.J., kept notes of these discussions while still interned in the camp, and he was able to save these notes after the collapse of the Third Reich. After the war, Schamoni and another former prisoner, Fr. Otto Pies, S.J., wrote about their experiences and in particular about a renewed diaconal order. I have written extensively elsewhere about this influence on the renewal of the diaconate; however, these discussions were wide-ranging and encompassed visions of reform that extended far beyond the diaconate. [9] Postwar theologians such as Karl Rahner and others would soon develop these ideas further and have a profound effect on the deliberations at the Council itself. Rahner's massive book on the possibility of a renewed and permanent diaconate, for example, was published in 1962 and made available to all of the Council fathers in that same year; it would have a direct impact on the Council's deliberations. [10] So, in a very real way, the horrific experience of those who endured those concentration camps found their way into St. Peter's in 1962.

In short, the average bishop would have experienced, in his own lifetime, two world wars, a worldwide economic collapse, the rise of totalitarian regimes, including Nazism, the Shoah, the initiation of the atomic age with the destruction of Hiroshima and Nagasaki, and the onset of a global Cold War. It is useful to recall that, less than a week after the Council's opening, the Cuban Missile Crisis took place. Earlier in the year both the Soviet Union and the United States detonated atmospheric nuclear tests; the civil rights movement in the United States and elsewhere was causing great social upheaval and

---

9. See, e.g., Otto Pies, "Block 26: Erfahrungen aus dem Priesterleben in Dachau," *Stimmen der Zeit* 141 (1947-1948): 10-28; Wilhelm Schamoni, *Familienväter als geweihte Diakone* (Paderborn: Schöningh, 1953). English trans., *Married Men as Ordained Deacons*, trans. Otto Eisner (London: Burns & Oates, 1955).

10. Karl Rahner and Herbert Vorgrimler, eds., *Diakonia in Christo: Über die Erneuerung des Diakonates* (Freiburg: Herder, 1962).

change, and around the world, countries were shaking off the coils of colonialism. In short, a new world was emerging following World War II, and the bishops in Council knew that the church must take action if she was to exercise any positive influence in these developments. As Pope John stated in his opening address, following his famous description of those around him who could see nothing but "prevarication and ruin":

> We feel we must disagree with those prophets of gloom, who are always forecasting disaster, as though the end of the world were at hand. In the present order of things, Divine Providence is leading us to a new order of human relations which, by men's own efforts and even beyond their very expectations, are directed toward the fulfillment of God's superior and inscrutable designs. And everything, even human differences, leads to the greater good of the Church.

The Second Vatican Council, therefore, was no simple gathering of church leaders (if the gathering of 2,600 bishops could ever be called "simple"!); it was, in effect, the opportunity for the pastoral leaders of the church to respond to World War II: the conditions that had led to that war and the world that emerged following that war. It was an opportunity for these leaders to chart a new course in human history, and such an opportunity demanded a *novus habitus mentis*: a new worldview, a new vision, a new horizon for the church and the world. The Council was not an end unto itself, but a courageous leap into the future. As Pope John concluded his opening address to his brother bishops, and indeed to the world, "The Council now beginning rises in the Church like daybreak, a forerunner of most splendid light. It is now only dawn."

Ordained Ministry: A New Way of Serving

We arrive now at our particular question for reflection: How might a new way of thinking affect our approach to the ordained ministries of the contemporary church? As theologian Susan Wood so aptly explains, "Ordained ministry arises from with the Church and reflects the structure of the Church. How we conceive of the Church will largely determine how we see ministry functioning within it."[11] Pope Paul VI offers the answer of the Council:

> We stress that the teaching of the Council is channeled in one direction, the service of humankind, of every condition, in every weakness and need. The Church has declared herself a servant of humanity at the very time when her teaching role and her pastoral government have, by reason of this Church solemnity, assumed greater splendor and vigor. However, the idea of service has been central.[12]

We are a servant church. What are the implications of this ecclesial self-identification on the possibilities for ordained ministry? Over the decades since the Council, considerable attention has been paid by theologians and canonists to the nature of ordination in the contemporary church. I wish to suggest two approaches to seeking a *novus habitus mentis* on ordination, one that considers a concrete historical example, and the other which draws from contemporary leadership theory. Both offer an opportunity to launch into a "new horizon" (to use Örsy's term) for ordained ministry.

Vatican II renewed many aspects of ordained ministry, especially with regard to the episcopate; in keeping with the "servant church" vision of the Council, the bishop's ministry is referred to as a *diakonia* of word, sacrament, and charity.[13] Presbyters and deacons participate in their own proper ways in this *diakonia* of the bishop. While there was not much attention paid directly to a theology of the presbyterate, the Council did authorize the renewal of a diaconate permanently exercised, even opening up the possibility of ordaining married men as deacons. Since we can track the progress of this renewal from its modern inception in the 1840s through the years of the Council, and the nearly fifty years of experience with the diaconate, it is possible to use this experience as a kind of limited paradigm for the renewal of other ordained ministries.

---

11. Susan K. Wood, *Sacramental Orders* (Collegeville, MN: Liturgical Press, 2000), 1.

12. Paul VI, *Hodie Concilium*, *Apostolicae sedis* 58 (1966): 57-64.

13. See *Lumen gentium* 24.

Much has been written about the details of the diaconate's renewal elsewhere, so I will not recount them here. [14] However, several highlights suggest themselves.

1. *Rationale and Configuration of a Renewed Order.* The renewal of the diaconate was based on the extensive pastoral needs identified, initially in Germany, during the nineteenth century. It received added focus in the Dachau concentration camp, as already discussed. In other words, the need to renew the diaconate was not based on some hypothetical construct but on pastoral need. Furthermore, the world's bishops decided that this need could be met by opening up the order of deacon to married as well as celibate men, even in the Latin church, where clerical celibacy had been the norm for more than a millennium.

2. *Variable Implementation.* During the conciliar discussions, Cardinal Suenens pointed out to the bishops that they need not implement the renewed diaconate in each and every diocese; rather, the diaconate would be an option available to those bishops who desired it. Later, in the United States, a similar process was followed: the United States Conference of Catholic Bishops (USCCB) requested and received authority to ordain permanent deacons in 1968. At the same time, the Conference determined that each diocesan bishop could make his own pastoral decision about implementing a permanent diaconate in his own diocese.

---

14. See, e.g., Bernard Cooke, *Ministry to Word and Sacraments* (Philadelphia: Fortress Press, 1976); Kenan B. Osborne, *Priesthood: A History of the Ordained Ministry in the Roman Catholic Church* (New York: Paulist Press, 1988); Kenan B. Osborne, *The Diaconate in the Christian Church* (Chicago: National Association of Diaconate Directors, 1996); William T. Ditewig, *The Emerging Diaconate: Servant Leaders in a Servant Church* (New York: Paulist Press, 2007); Nathan Mitchell, *Mission and Ministry: History and Theology in the Sacrament of Order* (Wilmington, DE: Michael Glazier, 1982); James M. Barnett, *The Diaconate: A Full and Equal Order*, rev. ed. (Valley Forge, PA: Trinity Press International, 1995); Joseph W. Pokusa, "A Canonical-Historical Study of the Diaconate in the Western Church" (JCD diss., Catholic University of America, 1979); Kenan B. Osborne, *The Permanent Diaconate: Its History and Place in the Sacrament of Orders* (Mahwah, NJ: Paulist Press, 2007).

3. *Diocesan-Based Formation.* Since the majority of deacon candidates are married, traditional seminary-style formation is neither feasible nor desirable, although there were initial attempts to do so. Instead, the USCCB has over the years developed national policies and standards for diocesan-based formation of deacons. This has resulted in considerable variation from diocese to diocese, based on the needs and resources of each diocese.

4. *Distinctive Theology of the Diaconate.* Ever since the ancient diaconate began its decline into a transitional state culminating in ordination to the presbyterate, any theological understanding of the diaconate was interpreted through the lens of the priesthood. This leads to misunderstandings about the nature of the diaconate, such as "the diaconate is only a partial form of the priesthood," or occasional references to "the lay deacon." Over the last decades, greater clarity in addressing the deacon's participation in the sacrament of Orders has highlighted the need to develop a proper theology of the diaconate distinct from the sacerdotal orders of presbyter and bishop.

5. *Restructuring the Sacrament of Orders.* The Council took several important steps with regard to the sacrament of Orders, leading Pope Paul VI to completely restructure the sacrament (in the Latin church) in 1972. He suppressed the rite of tonsure which had brought a man into the clerical state; he also suppressed the four minor orders (while retaining lector and acolyte as lay ministries, no longer ordinations) and the major order of subdeacon. In short, the sacrament of Orders was shown to be flexible and adaptable to emergent conditions.

What if we applied some of these same points to other orders or forms of ministry? For example: What we have learned is that not every order is alike, nor do they need to follow the same patterns of service. Different theologies already exist for the diaconal order and the sacerdotal orders; might other orders and ministries be included (again) within the sacrament of Orders? How is the sacramental significance of ordination to be understood in the contemporary church? History demonstrates, for example, that the meaning of ordination shifted radically in the twelfth century; how might a similar develop-

ment benefit the church today?[15] Selection and formation for the presbyterate might also be handled differently, using national standards
(which is already done) but tailored more explicitly to diocesan needs
and resources, adding greater availability and adaptability. Experience
has also shown, both in the Eastern and Latin traditions of the church,
that Matrimony and Orders are not merely compatible but mutually
beneficial. That is, for those called to both matrimony and orders, each
sacrament supports and informs the other; for those called to celibacy
as well as orders, such a pattern is also mutually beneficial. Might this
experience lead to other choices for the other orders?

However, one could say that all of these questions rest within our
current horizon. What other possibilities might still exist?

Zero-based leadership theory offers a potentially fruitful source
for deeper reflection. Essentially, this technique asks us to make no
assumptions but to base decisions on the facts presented. In a sense,
this approach is the opposite of the "we've always done it this way"
argument. Such an approach would undoubtedly not only lead to
ongoing reform of the existing orders but suggest further developments as well. We can see elements of this approach at work in the
ministry of Pope Francis.

Consider just one example from the early days of his pontificate.
Pope Francis met with young students from Jesuit schools in Italy and
Albania. As the pope prepared to give his five-page prepared speech,
he made the decision on the spot to change directions, to adapt to his
audience. He referred to his prepared text as "long and a little boring,"
looked at his watch, and said, "Let's do something different." He then
took spontaneous questions from a number of the students, answered
them frankly, and then jumped up to greet each of questioners with
an embrace and a kiss, returning to his chair for the next question.
As he gave a "little summary" of his prepared text, he spoke of the
balance that educators and parents must find in combining "security"
in education with "risk": that there is always the reaching out into the
unknown. He found a creative way to do exactly what he was chal-

---

15. One of the more recent histories of this paradigm shift of meaning may
be found in Gary Macy, *The Hidden History of Women's Ordination: Female Clergy
in the Medieval West* (New York: Oxford University Press, 2008).

lenging these students, their teachers, and their parents to do. He left the security of the prepared text and scripted event, took a risk, and made himself vulnerable to the impossible-to-predict nature of the questions these young people might ask. "Don't always be in the place of security."

The pope describes a similar visionary process in his Apostolic Exhortation *Evangelii gaudium* (*EG*).[16] It is a road map of sorts offering insights into his leadership vision for the church. Early in the document, Pope Francis addresses "Pastoral Activity and Conversion." In several paragraphs may be discerned a kind of zero-based review for institutional reform. It may very well be that the structural reforms being suggested here might wind up being the very heart of the document itself. In reviewing the pope's words, we might ask how they might affect ways in which the structures of ordained ministry may themselves be reformed.

> I hope that all communities will devote the necessary effort to advancing along the path of a pastoral and missionary conversion which cannot leave things as they presently are. "Mere administration" can no longer be enough. Throughout the world, let us be "permanently in a state of mission."[17]

For Pope Francis, all renewal in the church must be assessed by how well the church is able to evangelize: that's the standard. If something helps us to be better evangelizers, fine; if it is holding us back from evangelizing or is distorting the message, it must be abandoned or changed.

> I dream of a "missionary option," that is, a missionary impulse capable of transforming everything.... The renewal of structures demanded by pastoral conversion can only be understood in this light: as part of an effort to make them more mission-oriented, to make ordinary pastoral activity on every level more inclusive and open, to inspire in pastoral workers a constant

---

16. Pope Francis, Apostolic Exhortation *Evangelii gaudium*, November 24, 2013, 1.

17. Ibid.

desire to go forth and in this way to elicit a positive response for
all those whom Jesus summons to friendship with himself.[18]

The pope applies this standard to parishes, other religious groups
and movements, and dioceses. He points out that a parish is a useful institution "precisely because it possesses great flexibility, it can
assume quite different contours depending on the openness and
missionary creativity of the pastor and the community." What if this
standard were applied to the structures of ordained ministries? Just as
the pastoral judgments of the bishops of Vatican II led Pope Paul to
reconfigure the sacrament in 1972, how might it be further designed
or reimagined in our contemporary church? What are the needs of
the church, and what do we need to do to meet those needs? It's that
simple: a new way of thinking that uses one criterion of assessment:
how do we meet the demands of our mission to proclaim the Good
News effectively to the word?

The pope is asking all members of the church to seek out new horizons for service and to be unafraid to dare new thoughts, a *novus habitus mentis* about who and how we serve.

Conclusion

The impact of the Second Vatican Council—the bishops, popes, *per-
iti*, observers—all who brought their "joys, hopes, anxieties and griefs"
to the Council—continues to form and inform the church today. Its
trajectories of renewal reach back long before the Council itself and
lead us into new horizons. Christ tells us to "put out into the deep"
without fear; the Spirit is with us. In the example of Pope Francis
can be heard the voices of those priest-prisoners in Dachau, the gentle
voice of John XXIII announcing the dawn of a new day in the church,
and the voices of all those women and men who serve in the name
of Christ and the church on the streets, in the prisons, hospitals and
nursing homes, and at the margins of society, covered with "the smell
of the sheep." Just as all of them dared to dream big, so too are we, for
ultimately, the call to a *novus habitus mentis* comes not from the church
but from Christ himself.

---

18. Ibid., 27.

11

The Primacy of Conscience, Vatican II, and Pope Francis
The Opportunity to Renew a Tradition

David E. DeCosse

Few theological ideas are more closely associated with the Second Vatican Council than the concept of conscience. And few aspects of this concept have proved more vexing to Catholicism in the post-conciliar years than the notion known as the "primacy of conscience." The theologian Brian Lewis has helpfully defined this notion as, "One must follow the sure judgment of conscience even when through no fault of one's own it is mistaken."[1] In this essay, I will sketch the status of the primacy of conscience at the Second Vatican Council, analyze Joseph Ratzinger's critical and decisive interpretation of that concept—an interpretation that shaped the hierarchical teaching office's position on conscience for the decades since the Council—and identify the new openness to the primacy of conscience in the papacy of Pope Francis.

Primacy of Conscience at the Second Vatican Council

Throughout John O'Malley's history of the Second Vatican Council, conscience appears as one of the key themes implicated in many of the great conciliar issues: the role of the laity, religious freedom, ecumenism; the authority of the pope, the collegiality of the pope in union with the bishops, the Roman Catholic Church's dialogue with mod-

---

1. Brian Lewis, "The Primacy of Conscience," *Australian eJournal of Theology* 6 (February 2006): 1.

ern world, and more. O'Malley calls "conscience" the "most impressive among interiority words" used at the Council. As such, conscience was a decisive piece of vocabulary that signaled—along with words like "collegiality" and "cooperation" and "charism"—the Council's break with an immediate past of top-down ecclesiastical rule and the Council's recovery of the interior dimension of the Christian life. In turn, the concept of conscience, O'Malley argues, played a major role in inspiring the Council's epochal and distinctive style of speech—pastoral, not juridical—reflective of the inner reality of persons.[2]

The problematic of conscience came to the Council from the world and from within the church. On one hand, the problematic was the dramatic betrayal or constraint of conscience in the face of twentieth-century dictatorships. The European church had lived through the horror of the Second World War, in which a country with a powerful Catholic population rejected the most fundamental values associated with conscience in favor of fomenting aggression and genocide throughout Europe. Moreover, the church in Communist countries faced an aggressive totalitarianism demanding the fealty of conscience in the face of overwhelming state power. But if the encounters with Fascism and Communism represented instances of conscience being betrayed or under siege, the experience of the church in democratic nations throughout the world during the twentieth century testified to the value of respect for each individual's freedom of conscience. In turn, worldwide reactions against colonialism—and, often, against the European Christianity that came with the colonial powers—raised up the reality of the dignity of the human conscience outside the old, familiar conceptual constructs of Western and Catholic thought.[3] While these external factors certainly forced the issue, the Council also took up the topic of conscience in response to imperatives internal to the church. Here especially the increasingly centralized authority and juridical character of the church emerging from what O'Malley calls the "long nineteenth century" in Catholicism played the decisive role: Given the extensive reach of papal authority and the

---

2. John W. O'Malley, *What Happened at Vatican II* (Cambridge, MA: Harvard University Press, 2010), 48-52.
3. O'Malley, *What Happened at Vatican II*, 89-92.

establishment of a more codified Catholicism, what room was left for the authority of conscience among the men and women of the church? In the eyes of the popes of the "long nineteenth century" (which, in O'Malley's telling, extends well into the papacies of the early and mid-twentieth century), the chief culprit was liberalism as both a political and philosophical phenomenon. Whether confronting the impudence of freedom of the press or the skepticism of historicist thought, Rome readily blamed what it considered liberalism's notion of freedom of conscience as a crucial conceptual source of the evils of the day.[4]

The two key conciliar documents in which the primacy of conscience receives most attention are *Gaudium et spes* (GS) and *Dignitatis humanae* (DH) (both documents are also the ones in which the theme of conscience in general is most fully addressed). Neither document offers an extended, explicit argument in favor of the primacy of conscience. Rather, both assume the legitimacy of a concept that had in fact long been part of the Catholic moral tradition (even if the concept had become attenuated in the manualist moral tradition associated with the "long nineteenth century").[5] *Gaudium et spes* drew on the concept of conscience as one way to establish the basis for the theme of the document: the dialogue between the church and the modern world. The Catholic may search her conscience and find there the common truth shared by all people of good will and of any worldview. Also, the conciliar document's eloquent, well-known passage on conscience evoked the interiority and encounter with transcendence that are the ground of the claim that conscience has primacy: "Conscience is the most secret core and sanctuary of a [person]. There he is alone with God, Whose voice echoes in his depths" (GS 16). The passage also raises the issue of primacy with its reference to the erroneous conscience: "Conscience frequently errs from invincible ignorance without losing its dignity" (GS 16). In *Dignitatis humanae*, the argument for the right to religious freedom is cast in part in terms of the significance of the primacy of conscience: "In all his activity a man is bound to follow his conscience in order that he may come to God, the end and purpose

---

4. Ibid., 53-89.

5. Linda Hogan, *Confronting the Truth: Conscience in the Catholic Tradition* (Mahwah, NJ: Paulist Press, 2000), 98.

of life" (*DH* 3). Because this is true, the document argues, men and women have a justified claim in civil society to be free from coercion in their innermost thoughts and free from restraint in the public, religious expression of such thoughts. By invoking the primacy of conscience, the church at the Council was rearticulating a moral tradition that was especially associated with theological luminaries such as Thomas Aquinas[6] and John Henry Cardinal Newman.[7] But while the rearticulation restored the prominence of a neglected doctrine, the effort was hardly an unqualified victory. Theologian Linda Hogan has argued that the most accurate reading of the entirety of the conciliar documents in fact reveals two contrasting concepts of conscience: the first favoring the primacy of conscience but the second linking the dignity of conscience to its observance of the objective moral order as defined by the hierarchical teaching office of the church. In the first view, the individual conscience is understood as the place of encounter with the divine law—an encounter made possible by an autonomous and responsible conscience discovering the good within a given situation. In the second view, the Catholic hierarchy mediates divine law to the lay conscience, which is required to obey the good as it is hierarchically defined but not to discern the good as it is experientially discovered.[8] In part, we can see the theological roots of these conflicting concepts of conscience in what historian Massimo Faggioli has called

---

6. When Thomas Aquinas argued in favor of the primacy of conscience by saying that "conscience always binds," he broke with established medieval traditions that argued either that conscience never binds or that conscience only obliges in its own right in morally indifferent situations. As Aquinas put it, "when erring reason proposes something as being commanded by God, then to scorn the dictate of reason is to scorn the commandment of God" (*Summa Theologica* I-II Q19, A5, ad 2). On the primacy of conscience, see, e.g., in the work of Aquinas, the entirety of *ST* I-II 19, 5 and 6, and *De veritate* Q17, 2, 3, 4, and 5.

7. Newman famously affirmed the primacy of conscience when he said, "Certainly, if I am obliged to bring religion into after-dinner toasts (which indeed does not seem quite the thing), I shall drink—to the Pope, if you please,—still, to Conscience first, and to the Pope afterwards" (Newman, "A Letter Addressed to His Grace the Duke of Norfolk on Occasion of Mr. Gladstone's Recent Expostulation," in *Conscience, Consensus, and the Development of Doctrine,* ed. James Gaffney (New York: Image Books, 1992), 457.

8. Hogan, *Confronting the Truth,* 109-15.

dueling neo-Thomist and Augustinian camps present at the Council and decisive in the interpretations of the postconciliar era.[9] Viewed in this light, the text of *Gaudium et spes* 16 stands as a high-water mark of the neo-Thomist wing's characteristic optimism: conscience not only has primacy but is also a place where men and women hear the echo of the voice of God and are able to detect the universal law of love binding all people together. It will next be helpful to see how the decisive criticism of *Gaudium et spes* 16 by one of the leaders of the Augustinian wing—theologian Joseph Ratzinger—laid down the terms by which the hierarchical teaching office has understood the primacy of conscience for the last decades.

Joseph Ratzinger and the Primacy of Conscience

In the depths of his conscience, man detects a law which he does not impose upon himself, but which holds him to obedience. Always summoning him to love good and avoid evil, the voice of conscience when necessary speaks to his heart: do this, shun that. For man has in his heart a law written by God; to obey it is the very dignity of man; according to it he will be judged. Conscience is the most secret core and sanctuary of a man. There he is alone with God, Whose voice echoes in his depths. In a wonderful manner conscience reveals that law which is fulfilled by love of God and neighbor. In fidelity to conscience, Christians are joined with the rest of men in the search for truth, and for the genuine solution to the numerous problems which arise in the life of individuals from social relationships. Hence the more right conscience holds sway, the more persons and groups turn aside from blind choice and strive to be guided by the objective norms of morality. Conscience frequently errs from invincible ignorance without losing its dignity. The same cannot be said for a man who cares but little for truth and goodness, or for a conscience which by degrees grows practically sightless as a result of habitual sin. (GS 16)

---

9. Massimo Faggioli, *Vatican II: The Battle for Meaning* (Mahwah, NJ: Paulist Press, 2000), 66-90.

In a commentary written shortly after the Council, Ratzinger argued that *Gaudium et spes* 16 used a "rather evasive formula"[10] in its account of the binding force of erroneous conscience. Chiefly, he argued, the document was mistakenly and "wholly modern"[11] in its failure to recognize the guilt attributable to an erroneous reason that does not but should know the demands of God's law. As Ratzinger saw it, a person may claim the binding force of an erroneous conscience. But such a claim may likely be clouded by self-deception and enclosed in a world of subjectivism. Here, in short, is the heart of Ratzinger's criticism of the primacy of conscience—a criticism that has prevailed as the point of view for the last decades of the hierarchical teaching office of the church (during the papacy of John Paul II in which Ratzinger served as head of the Congregation for the Doctrine of the Faith and during Ratzinger's tenure himself as Pope Benedict XVI). To be sure, the primacy of conscience is generally affirmed: It is wrong to act contrary to the judgment of one's conscience, whether one's conscience is correct or erroneous. But the primacy is also either denied outright or highly conditioned. In any case, the onus has shifted. Where *Gaudium et spes* 16 sought to rearticulate the tradition of the primacy of conscience and put the burden on those who would question it, Ratzinger in the last decades has taken the rearticulated tradition and put the burden heavily back on the shoulders of those who invoke it.

Thus Ratzinger argued that *Gaudium et spes* 16 offered an "insufficient account . . . of the limits of conscience."[12] On the one hand, the conciliar document rightly affirmed the sacred character of conscience as a place of encounter with the divine. The passage also correctly noted the capacity of conscience to know and be bound by the objective moral law. And the text reaffirmed the long-standing doctrine that the erroneous conscience could without culpability retain its dignity. For Ratzinger, however, these ways of putting things were accurate

---

10. Joseph Ratzinger, "The Dignity of the Human Person," in *Commentary on the Documents of Vatican II: Volume 5, Pastoral Constitution on the Church in the Modern World,* ed. Herbert Vorgrimler (New York: Herder & Herder, 1969), 136.

11. Ibid.

12. Ibid.

only insofar as they went. All needed substantial qualification—especially in terms of a doctrine of sin. Thus, he argued, the passage would benefit from the incorporation of the abiding principles laid down in the first chapters of the Letter to the Romans: that a pervasive and enduring human wickedness has prevented the human conscience in every generation from recognizing what it should—the sovereign authority of God and the demands of the moral law.[13]

> Ever since the creation of the world his invisible nature, namely, his eternal power and deity, has been clearly perceived in the things that have been made. So they are without excuse; for although they knew God they did not honor him as God or give thanks to him, but they became futile in their thinking and their senseless minds were darkened. (Romans 1:20-21)

This phenomenon of blindness is not something occasional, as the conciliar passage suggests. Rather, for Ratzinger, it is an enduring aspect of the human condition without reference to which *Gaudium et spes* 16 fails a crucial theological litmus test.

And the effects of this failure, as Ratzinger saw it, rippled throughout the passage. The claim in the conciliar text that in conscience one encounters the divine leaves unexplained how one's conscience, attuned to the truth of God, could also therefore possibly be mistaken. Similarly, the assertion in the text that conscience is capable of recognizing the objective moral law, while true, was naïve about the ways that human willfulness can obscure the claims of the commandments. Lastly, the "rather evasive formula" of the passage about the erroneous conscience suffered from a similar naïveté. But here Ratzinger takes his argument beyond the criticism of the conciliar passage itself to the bold claim—disputed by other scholars—that the concept of the binding nature of the erroneous conscience in Aquinas was "nullified" because Aquinas himself was "convinced that error is culpable."[14]

---

13. Ibid., 135.

14. Ibid., 136. For a nuanced view of Aquinas on the erroneous conscience and culpability, see Eric D'Arcy, *Conscience and Its Right to Freedom* (New York: Sheed & Ward, 1961).

We can see the same critical themes about the primacy of conscience elaborated in Ratzinger's widely recognized later essay "Conscience and Truth." To be sure, he again affirms there the "undisputed"[15] doctrinal point: "one must follow a certain conscience—or at least not act against it."[16] But he also paints a dark portrait of the contemporary appropriation of the primacy of conscience in church and culture. In effect, he lumps those within the church favoring what he calls a "morality of conscience" with the surrounding secular and liberal culture that understands such a morality in terms of a pervasive subjectivism. Within the church, Ratzinger argues, those favoring a morality of conscience have falsely and starkly set themselves against a "morality of authority" (they have even pejoratively confined the latter to the preconciliar church).[17] But, in doing so, the advocates of the morality of conscience have in fact subscribed to the reigning liberal ethos in which the principle of the primacy of conscience properly considered has become the principle of conscience understood as a law entirely unto itself. Thus, Ratzinger argues, this liberal concept of conscience suffers from an assumption that it is always right or infallible or wholly self-authenticating.[18] But this high degree of subjective sway presents a philosophical and empirical problem. If each person's conscience is oriented to a singular, unassailable truth, then each person is no longer able to affirm the common truths binding people together and making possible life in society. It is important to note how deep Ratzinger's criticism here goes. The advocates of the morality of conscience are "[dispensing] with truth" and thus rendering conscience helplessly prone to the logic of subjectivity and pliable to the demands of social conformity.[19] Amid such powerful cultural forces, the word "conscience" is emptied of meaning and becomes "a euphemistic way of saying that there is no such thing as an actual conscience, conscience understood as a 'co-knowing' with the truth."[20]

---

15. Joseph Ratzinger, "Conscience in Truth," in *Crisis of Conscience*, ed. John M. Haas (New York: Crossroad, 1996), 2.

16. Ibid.

17. Ibid., 1-2.

18. Ibid., 2.

19. Ibid., 3.

20. Ibid., 10.

Beyond a philosophical and cultural criticism, the doctrine of sin again plays a crucial part in Ratzinger's effort in this essay to circumscribe sharply the primacy of conscience. Thus he considers the problem in light of members of the Nazi SS during the time of the Third Reich. Given the validity of the concept of the primacy of conscience, does that mean that members of the SS who murdered in a way consistent with their objectively wrong consciences are in fact saved? Ratzinger regards this possibility as absurd and deploys the absurdity of the example against what he regards as the too-common and casual appeal to the authority of a firm, subjective certitude of conscience. And here the doctrine of sin supplies the missing piece of this puzzle. The capacity to recognize guilt, Ratzinger argues, belongs to the spiritual constitution of persons. Moreover, this capacity must stand as a sentinel before the present and the past. We may be aware of the guilt consciously connected to wrongdoing we know now. But we must also be vigilant in the face of the more obscure guilt connected to misdeeds that we have long forgotten or deliberately put out of mind. "Cleanse thou me from my unknown faults" (Psalm 19:13), the psalmist says (and Ratzinger quotes approvingly). The certain conscience of the member of the SS was bought at the price of banishing from consciousness what was surely the guilt arising from the objectively wrong and murderous hatred of Jews.[21] Here again for Ratzinger the Letter to the Romans supplies the theological framework tying the cultural and psychological analysis together. The SS may be an extreme example but they stand in a continuum with the condition of humanity, which on account of its very creaturehood ought to recognize in conscience the existence of God and the claims of the moral law. In Paul's telling in Romans 1, there is no appeal possible to the primacy of conscience against this fundamental demand on humanity: No one may be excused. Or, as Ratzinger says of this section of Romans (and as he applies to his critique of the primacy of conscience in church and society), "The whole theory of salvation through ignorance breaks apart with this verse."[22]

---

21. Ibid., 4-6.
22. Ibid., 6.

But what to do to vindicate the primacy of conscience in the face of criticisms that the doctrine in its common practice in the church is mired in subjectivism and in the known and unknown depths of sin? Ratzinger offers two conditions within which the concept should be embedded. The first is what he calls the "ontological level of the phenomenon [which] consists in the fact that something like an original memory of the good and true ... has been implanted in us."[23] The Catholic moral tradition has called this level of conscience *synderesis*. Ratzinger proposes replacing the term *synderesis* with the Platonic term *anamnesis*, or memory. By this proposal, he signals the significance of an already-present "basic understanding of the good" and of an "inner sense, a capacity to recall, so that the one whom it addresses, if he is not turned in on himself, hears its echo from within."[24] Any claims for primacy can never be detached from such conditions. Moreover, these given, ontological conditions make evident to human knowledge "the essential constants of the will of God" in the commandments, which can in principle be found and elucidated in all cultures.[25] This, then, is the anamnesis of creation. To it, Ratzinger joins the anamnesis of faith understood as the sureness of the Christian memory resident in the body of Christ. The power of such recollection is especially resident in the "simple faith which leads to the discernment of spirits." But such "simple faith" still requires defense by the pope from the destruction "threatened by a subjectivity forgetful of its own foundation as well as by the pressures of social and cultural conformity."[26]

The specification of anamnesis is, then, the first condition within which the concept of the primacy of conscience is to be embedded. The second condition pertains to conscience as an act of judgment about something to be done or that has been done. Here Ratzinger insists that the rationality appropriate to the judgment of conscience is not a matter merely of detached logic or technique. Rather, he argues, our reason and will are profoundly interconnected. Even more, our

---

23. Ibid., 13.
24. Ibid.
25. Ibid., 14.
26. Ibid., 15.

capacity to recognize something as true and obligatory depends on our will and the choices that have shaped an already-formed moral character, for good or for ill. It is never wrong to heed the convictions of one's conscience, Ratzinger notes. But it may have been wrong to have come to such convictions in the first place.[27]

Here we can see the basic elements of Ratzinger's powerful critique of the primacy of conscience—a critique replicated often in the last decades in the documents of the hierarchical teaching office. Ratzinger's critique has firmly and persuasively placed the doctrine of the primacy of conscience within a rich, ontological texture and within the powerful effect of the doctrine of sin. Even while rooting the doctrine on an ontological basis, the focus throughout is moral and ethical. But several crucial shortcomings of his critique should be noted. First, the critique construes conscience largely in terms of conservation, the past, memory—but not in terms of conscience as a place of encounter with what is new. Second, the content of the past to which conscience should be oriented is understood chiefly and univocally in terms of truth and the moral law (with the universality of the moral law being indicative of objective truth). But this way of putting things does not, for instance, distinguish between primary and secondary precepts of the moral law nor does it entertain very much the complexity of identifying the moral law in markedly different cultural contexts (and thus, correspondingly, has a diminished role for prudence in the doctrine of conscience). Because it does not identify these obvious complexities, Ratzinger's critique is able far too easily to assume that people are guilty for not knowing the moral law when in fact they may be inculpably unaware of it. With such a ready assumption of guilt, we see a sharp shift from *Gaudium et spes* 16. Where the conciliar document spoke of people's consciences "not infrequently" in a state of inculpable ignorance, Ratzinger's writings assume that people are often guilty for such ignorance. Or, as the theologian Brian Johnstone described the profound shift from the time of *Gaudium et spes* 16 to the papacies of John Paul II and Benedict XVI, The "difference can be stated succinctly: Christians are

---

27. Ibid., 15-16.

often ignorant, but inculpably so; Christians are ignorant, but often culpably so."[28] A final difficulty with Ratzinger's critique is that the "sureness of the Christian memory" constitutive of anamnesis is not so much associated with something like Cardinal Newman's more participatory sense of the faithful intuition of the laity (as Newman articulated the notion in *On Consulting the Faithful in Matters of Doctrine*) as it is with the defensive role of the hierarchical teaching office in guaranteeing the unchanging perpetuity of such memory. Thus, the theologian Jayne Hoose has criticized how Ratzinger's constrained view of the primacy of conscience played a role in major recent documents of the hierarchical teaching office such as *Veritatis splendor* and the *Catechism of the Catholic Church*. In the former, Hoose argues, the approach of the encyclical "asserts the authority of the Magisterium and a submissive model of conscience, apparently claiming that personal conscience and reason cannot be set in opposition to the teaching of the Magisterium.[29]" In the latter document, Hoose similarly argues that "a search for truth by the conscience . . . can only result in submitting to the truth as interpreted by the Magisterium."[30]

Primacy of Conscience and the Renewal of a Tradition

The thirteenth century witnessed rival theological schools contesting the meaning of the primacy of conscience. Some argued that there was no such thing; that conscience at most teaches and encourages but never obliges. Others, like Bonaventure, argued that conscience is bound by matters that are good or evil in themselves but not by indifferent things. Thomas Aquinas emphasized the privileged place occupied by human reason in mediating obligation to conscience.[31] I note this range of thirteenth-century views of the primacy of con-

---

28. Brian V. Johnstone, "Conscience in Error," in *Conscience: Readings in Moral Theology* 14, ed. Charles Curran (Mahwah, NJ: Paulist Press, 2004), 169.

29. Jayne Hoose, "Conscience in *Veritatis Splendor* and the *Catechism*," *Conscience: Readings in Moral Theology* 14, ed. Charles Curran (Mahwah, NJ: Paulist Press, 2004), 91.

30. Ibid., 93.

31. D'Arcy, *Conscience*, 80-87.

science because it provides a helpful analogue to the present day and the advent of Pope Francis's papacy.

In short, within Catholicism there have long been different schools of thought about the primacy of conscience; and, in the more favorable view of the primacy of conscience articulated thus far by Francis, we are seeing a conflict of schools emerging. Such a conflict was immediately evident after an interview with a noted Italian atheist in which Francis said that "the question for those who do not believe in God is to abide by their own conscience. There is sin, also for those who have no faith, in going against one's conscience."[32] Here the pope articulated anew the doctrine of the primacy of conscience but did so by departing from the Ratzinger-inspired formula that emphasized the culpability of the conscience for failing to know God. The criticism of Francis by Catholics familiar with the view of conscience of the last papacies was swift and sharp and echoed the language of the last years: The new pope was promoting a "subjective definition of conscience."[33]

But additional comments by Francis have made clearer the direction of his thought in this matter: He is seeking to move beyond the last decades' more exclusive emphasis on conscience and morality and instead recover the foundation of the primacy of conscience in the relationship to the divine. Or, as *Gaudium et spes* 16 famously put it, he is seeking to restore an emphasis on conscience understood as the "most secret core and sanctuary of [a person]." This new emphasis was most evident in a response he gave in a long interview with a Jesuit journal to a question about how the Society of Jesus could serve the church today. Francis did not lay out a program of desirable moral action. Rather, he spoke of the need, so to speak, for living in a style of tension. One must affirm Christ, the church, the moral law, what is immediately before us to be done. But one must always hold those goods in tension with the "*Deus semper maior*, the always-greater God,

---

32. Lizzy Davies, "Pope Francis Tells Atheists to Abide by Their Own Consciences," *The Guardian* (September 11, 2013).

33. *New Oxford Review*. New Oxford Notes: "Pope Francis & the Primacy of Conscience," (December 2013).

and the pursuit of the ever-greater glory of God."[34] The thing that mediates this tension is conscience in which what is given from the past may be surmounted by what is demanded for the future by the always-greater God. Here Francis reimagines richly both the moral and the transcendent dimensions of conscience. The subjectivist moral threat of the primacy of conscience recedes from view. The mystery of divine love that is the basis of the claim to primacy returns to its rightful place in the drama.

---

34. Antonio Spadaro, "A Big Heart Open to God: The Exclusive Interview with Pope Francis," *America* (September 30, 2013).

EPILOGUE

Sensus fidelium

ALBERT GELPI AND BARBARA CHARLESWORTH GELPI

In terms of far-reaching implications and consequences across the entire life of the church, the most radical declaration of the Second Vatican Council is its definition of the church as the people of God: not the monarchical and totalitarian structure that the church had developed in imitation of imperial Rome and then of medieval feudalism; not the vertical structure in which power was invested in a single monarch, his authority divinely ordained, who, with his court ("Curia" means "court"), rules over obedient lay subjects. Jesus neither established nor, we suspect, favored any such structure for the church; it is a historical development, understandable and easily explained. And thus changeable. The church as the people of God is a radical conception in the sense that it operates from the root of the church's complex structure, from the very conception of the church as a living body.

In *What Happened at Vatican II*, cited often in this book, John O'Malley reminds us that there had never been so large and representative a gathering as this Council—not just in the history of the church but in the history of humankind. Vatican I had declared the primacy and *ex cathedra* authority of the pope, thus consolidating the process of centralizing power and authority in the Vatican that had been developing—not without resistance but with steady advance—for centuries. However, almost a century after Vatican I, *Lumen gentium* (*LG*), the Dogmatic Constitution on the Church, was approved and promulgated on November 21, 1964, with only five dissenting votes from the assembled bishops of the church. Its first chapter on "The Mystery of the Church" begins with its intention "to declare with greater clarity to the faithful and the entire human race the nature of

170

the church and its universal mission" (*LG* 1).[1] Without countervening in any way what Vatican I had said about papal authority, the second chapter, on "The People of God," declares that all the faithful share "in the one priesthood of Christ" and "in the prophetic role of Christ" (*LG* 9, 12). Indeed, while maintaining that the people of God are "under the guidance of the sacred magisterium to which it is faithfully obedient," *Lumen gentium* makes this empowering statement:

> The universal body of the faithful who have received the anointing of the holy one (see 1 Jn 2,20 and 27), cannot be mistaken in belief. It displays this particular quality through a supernatural sense of the faith in the whole people when "from the bishops to the last of the faithful laity," it expresses the consent of all in the matters of faith and morals. (*LG* 12)

The teaching authority of the magisterium is associated with the obedience and consent of the faithful.

Only after defining the church as the entire people of God does *Lumen gentium* define the specific roles of the bishops and of the laity in the life and mission of the church. Chapter 3 affirms the collegiality of bishops with the pope in the authority of the church and its charism of infallibility. Chapter 4 addresses the laity's "special character which is secular": "It is the special vocation of the laity to seek the kingdom of God by engaging in temporal affairs and ordering these in accordance with the will of God," so that "the power of the gospel may shine forth in the daily life of the family and society" and "so that the mission of the Church may be more able to meet the particular needs of the modern world" (*LG* 31, 35, 36). To that end, "in accordance with the knowledge, competence or authority that they possess, they [laypeople] have the right and indeed sometimes the duty to make known their opinions on matters which concern the good of the Church," and pastors "should willingly make use of their prudent counsel" (*LG* 37).

Dignitatis humanae (*DH*), the Council document that endorsed unhesitatingly the right to religious freedom, marked a distinct shift in the church's attitude toward other religions, but its declarations about

---

1. All citations of the Council herein are taken from Norman Tanner, *Vatican II: The Essential Texts* (New York: Image Books, 2012).

freedom of conscience for those outside the church inescapably had resonance for the newly empowered laity within the church. Here are its opening words:

> The dignity of the human person is a concern of which people of our time are becoming increasingly more aware. In growing numbers they demand that they should enjoy the use of their own responsible judgment and freedom, and decide on their actions on grounds of duty and conscience, without external pressure or coercion. (*DH* 1)

This principle meant that "no one should be forced to act against his conscience in religious matters, nor prevented from acting according to his conscience . . ." (*DH* 2). Moreover, the sixteenth section of *Gaudium et spes* (GS), the Pastoral Constitution on the Church in the Modern World, pronounced this unyielding defense of "the dignity of the moral conscience":

> Deep within their conscience individuals discover a law which they do not make for themselves but which they are bound to obey, whose voice, ever summoning them to love what is good and to avoid what is evil, rings in their heart when necessary with the command: Do this, keep away from that. For inscribed in their hearts by God, human beings have a law whose observance is their dignity and in accordance with which they are to be judged. Conscience is the most intimate center and sanctuary of a person, in which he or she is alone with God whose voice echoes within them. (*GS* 16)

The theology of Vatican II, articulated in its promulgated documents, calls the whole of God's people—cleric and lay, bishop and priest, each and all of us, individually and in community—to incarnate God's word in our personal lives and express it in the network of relationships that constitute community and society. This difficult process of conversion is how we work to realize the Reign of God on earth, as we pray each day in the Lord's Prayer. What's more, the conception of the church as the people of God, as we have seen, raises the tricky and by no means settled issue of whether any teaching has final and binding authority without what theologians call the *sensus fidelium*, the assent of the informed and conscientious faithful to that teaching. We are only just beginning to test out what the empowerment of the laity, initiated by the Council, means and entails. However, there can be no question that the revisioning of the church in the modern world requires a decentralization and sharing of authority, a democratization and sharing of responsibility, a call to personal holiness and societal conversion, a trust in the power of the Holy Spirit to inform the souls and consciences of all God's people. Predictably the forces of distrust and retraction began to subvert both the Council's teachings and the Council's spirit by reasserting papal and curial authority— first with the interventions of Paul VI during the last sessions of the Council and afterwards, more systematically and harshly, by John Paul II and Benedict XVI and the reactionary bishops they appointed.

Nonetheless, the winds of change continue to blow through the window that Good Pope John opened. How, then, are we Catholics expressing and realizing the responsibility of our empowerment? The data and reflection and analysis on what contemporary Catholics believe indicate that the essentials of the faith—proclaimed in the Gospels and the New Testament, articulated in the Creed, and maintained through the centuries—are unshaken and unshakable: belief in a personal and loving God, in the redemptive life and death of Jesus, in the vitality of the sacraments and particularly of the Eucharist, in the necessity of individual prayer and church community, in the cause of peace and social justice. But an ever-growing number of informed and conscientious Catholics dissent from official teaching of the magisterium about restrictions and prohibitions in a number of areas, mostly concerning sexuality in one way or another: clerical celibacy, women's ordination, contraception, divorce and remarriage, homosexuality, same-sex marriage. None of these matters affect the Creed we Catholics all profess, and many of us, including priests and theologians (and perhaps even a few bishops?), are claiming conscientious dissent in one or more or all of those areas and are calling for a rethinking and a change in official teaching, just as the church has evolved in its teaching on other issues over time and through history. Meanwhile, despite stiff resistance from the Vatican and from many American bishops, statistical data indicate that the *sensus fidelium*, the sense of the faithful, on these issues has begun to coalesce and express itself.

Before their papacy both John Paul and Benedict had been involved in discussions at Vatican II—and not always happy about the direction of the discussions. As many commentators have observed, Francis is the first postconciliar pope, and in his recent interviews he seems eager to affirm and extend even the most radical teachings of Vatican II. About the primacy of the individual's conscience Francis told Eugenio Scalfari, in an interview in *La Repubblica* on October 1, 2013: "Each of us has a vision of good and evil. . . . Everyone has his own idea of good and evil and must choose to follow the good and fight evil as he conceives them." In another interview with Antonio Spadaro, S.J., published in the United States in the September 30, 2103, issue of *America*, the church as the people of God leads Francis to extend the infallibility of the church to include the *sensus fidelium*. Here is his remarkable statement, quoted earlier in this book:

> And the Church is the people of God on the journey through history, with joys and sorrows. Thinking with the Church, therefore, is my way of being a part of this people. And all the faithful, considered as a whole, are infallible in matters of belief, and the people display this *infallibilitas in credendo*, this infallibility in believing, through a supernatural sense of the faith of all the people walking together. This is what I understand today as the "thinking with the Church" of which St. Ignatius speaks. When the dialogue among the people and the bishops and the pope goes down this road and is genuine, then it is assisted by the Holy Spirit. So this thinking with the Church does not concern the theologians only. . . . We should not even think, therefore, that "thinking with the Church" means only thinking with the hierarchy of the Church.

The pope as part of the people of God; the dialogue among people and bishops and pope; the people's *infallibilitas in credendo*; the shared faith informed by the Holy Spirit: Francis's words transform a Vatican I church into a Vatican II church in our journey through history to the Beatific Vision.

* * * *

The lengthy "Apostolic Exhortation" by Pope Francis, promulgated on November 24, 2013, under the title *Evangelii gaudium* (*EG*), reiterates and enlarges on a number of the themes and concerns expressed in earlier interviews and in papal homilies, including that of the church, the people of God, as an "evangelizing community" on pilgrimage together. On that journey, a bishop at times "will sometimes go before his people, pointing their way and keeping their hope vibrant"; at others "he will simply be in their midst with his unassuming and merciful presence"; and "yet at other times, he will have to walk after them, helping those who lag behind and—above all—allowing the flock to strike out on new paths" (*EG* 31).

As bishop of Rome, Pope Francis has himself served as model for the first and second positions to be taken by an episcopal shepherd. He has constantly by word and example urged the way forward to a greater awareness of the priority that Vatican II, following the call of the gospel, gave to concern for the poor, and he has found ways in which to make his own "unassuming and merciful presence" felt among all the faithful. He has also been seen in the third position: behind the flock, searching out those, such as Eugenio Scalfari, who have taken other paths. But how are we to understand what is meant by the counsel, emphasized by the phrase "above all," that the bishop also allow the flock "to strike out on new paths," thus taking the lead while he walks behind?

The pastoral metaphor breaks down at this point because while sheep, with their nimbler feet and better sense of smell than their shepherd, might create a well-advised shortcut to new pastures, the laity and the clergy of the church—the people of God—face immeasurably more complex issues during their long journey. One needs, therefore, to consider what institutional structures are in place that would make it possible for members of the laity to offer opinions about what direction might be best in order to achieve the common goal: experiencing the reality of God's love for oneself and manifesting that love to others. The answer at this point has to be, there are none. There were laypersons—proportionally a very few men and far, far fewer women—who were allowed to witness the sessions of Vatican

II, but none had the right to vote on the issues discussed there, much less the privilege of initiating topics or suggesting "new paths."

Pope Francis, intent as he clearly is on implementing the doctrines promulgated by Vatican II, has meditated on this very issue. He begins section 102 of *Evangelii gaudium* by recalling the language of the Council, when he writes: "Lay people are, put simply, the vast majority of the people of God." He continues, using surprise as a wise pedagogue might do, to catch the attention of his readers: "The minority—ordained ministers—are at their service." As the paragraph continues, however, the focus changes from the "service" asked from ordained ministers to that asked from members of the laity by virtue of their "mission": "a deeply rooted sense of community and great fidelity to the tasks of charity, catechesis, and the celebration of faith." The pope then pauses to note two reasons for a muted awareness of this lay responsibility in many places. In some, referring perhaps to situations where congregations are in need of greater educational opportunities, laypeople "have not been given the formation needed to take on important responsibilities." But in others, where the lay members do have access to the formation and training needed, "it is because in their particular churches room has not been made for them to speak and to act, due to an excessive clericalism that keeps them away from decision-making" (EG 102).

Decision making: startling words. And as the paragraph moves toward its conclusion, it seems as if Pope Francis is thinking of lay Catholics as each dedicated to a mission within his or her chosen field in order to further "the evangelization of professional and intellectual life" described as a "significant pastoral challenge."

Concern about the laity's involvement in transforming the "social, political, and economic sectors" of society makes it necessary that the pope step, in paragraph 103, into the mined terrain of women's status in the church. He makes a somewhat awkward first step by a seemingly essentialist focus on women's contribution to society as based in "the sensitivity, intuition and other distinctive skill sets which they, more than men, tend to possess." The question is whether women possess these qualities inherently or whether the skills have emerged, sometimes literally as survival strategies, through eons of male domination. And just as men's potential for a sensitive awareness of others' needs and motivations can be either fostered by use or truncated when considered women's work, so women's capacity for leadership in any number of areas can be actualized only by being given the opportunity to make itself manifest. Later in the paragraph the word "incisive," associated as it is with the process of decision making, suggests that Pope Francis himself acknowledges women's potential for leadership: "[W]e need to create still broader opportunities for a more incisive female presence in the Church." And in the next sentence he underscores that point. He quotes from paragraph 295 of the 2006 *Compendium of the Social Doctrine of the Church*, which states (though again in essentialist terms) that since "the feminine genius is needed in all expressions in the life of society, the presence of women must also be guaranteed in the work place," but he continues and concludes that sentence with a significant clause of his own: "and in the various other settings where important decisions are made, both in the Church and in social structures" (*EG* 103). Again, the pope appears to be turning over in thought the question of how better to include laypersons, women as well as men, in at least some of the church's decision making. But what present structures might be adapted to that purpose, or what future ones created?

Women's omnipresence in the work of the church—both as religious involved in teaching, nursing, social work, and care giving of many kinds, and as laywomen undertaking a wide variety of diocesan and parish tasks and duties—is undeniable but can also be rendered as invisible as that of servants in a Jane Austen novel. While Vatican II made the hugely significant step of reestablishing the diaconate as a "proper and permanent rank in the hierarchy" rather than the stage on the way to priestly ordination that it had become since the twelfth century and opened it to men, including those "living in the married state" (*LG* 29), it made no provision for any change that would better include women within the hierarchical structures of the church. Nonetheless, the restoration of the diaconate for laymen, the hope for ongoing change promised by that and other accomplishments of Vatican II, and the huge energy engendered by the women's movement that began shortly after Vatican II ended, created a rising expectation in the early 1970s that women who felt called to serve as deacons or even as priests might have their sense of vocation honored.

Such thinking received a strong response in the *Declaration on the Question of the Admission of Women to the Ministerial Priesthood* promulgated on October 15, 1976, fairly close to the end of Paul VI's pontificate. The document laid out at length the lack of any historical precedent for women presiding at the liturgy, but the culminating argument, given in section 5, turned on the inadequacy of women's bodies: "[T]he priest is a [sacramental] sign, the supernatural effectiveness of which comes from the ordination received, but a sign that must be perceptible and which the faithful must recognize with ease.... There would not be this 'natural resemblance' which must exist between Christ and his minister if the role of Christ were not taken by a man.... For Christ himself was and remains a man."

Many among both the clergy and the laity disputed the terms of that argument, however, and discussions about the possibility of women's ordination continued, muted perhaps but unabated, until 1994, when John Paul II issued a declaration that "the Church has no authority whatsoever to confer priestly ordination on women," adding that "this judgment is to be definitively held by all the Church's faithful." The clear intention was to take the topic "off the table."

Twenty years have passed, and though the topic did not actually disappear at all—a revelatory book like Gary Macy's *The Hidden History of Women's Ordination* was published in 2007—there could be no further *official* consideration, were it not that Pope Francis himself, as another of his many surprises, alludes to it in paragraph 104 of *Evangelii gaudium* in the following terms: "The reservation of the priesthood to males, as a sign of Christ the Spouse who gives himself in the Eucharist, is not a question open to discussion, but it can prove especially divisive if a sacramental power is too closely identified with power in general."

Now, a quick reading of Francis's words might suggest that he is simply restating John Paul II's injunction against mention of the topic, but of course by his very reference to this "closed" issue, he reopens it as only he, as pope, has technically the authority to do. More than that, he reopens the old argument against women's ordination in order to critique it, first of all by calling it "divisive," and then by holding up the corollary to it, the one that identifies a priest's sacramental power with "power in general" as "especially divisive."

An example of that identification between sacramental power and power in general comes at the end of the same section 5 in the 1976 *Declaration* that only a male body can represent Christ. It urges the faithful "to study in greater detail the meaning of the episcopate and the priesthood, and to rediscover the real and preeminent place of the priest in the community of the baptized, of which he indeed forms a part but from which he is distinguished because, in the actions that call for the character of ordination, for the community he is ... the image of Christ himself." While not making specific allusion to that now distant statement, Pope Francis takes pains to warn against the hierarchicalism and clericalism it exemplifies. He writes, "The configuration of the priest to Christ the head—namely as the principal source of grace—does not imply an exaltation which would set him above others," adding also that the "key and axis" of ministerial priesthood is "not power understood as domination, but the power to administer the sacrament of the Eucharist; this is the origin of its authority, which is always a service to God's people" (*EG* 104).

The sentence that immediately follows—the last sentence in the paragraph as well as the last related to the topic of women, since *Evangelii gaudium* moves on in paragraph 105 to a consideration of youth ministry—is highly significant but also somewhat puzzling through its use twice of the pronoun "this": "This presents a great challenge for pastors and theologians, who are in a position to recognize more fully what this entails with regard to the possible role of women in decision making in different areas of the Church's life." The first "this" appears to refer back to a tendency to conflate sacramental with institutional power, the "challenge" being to keep them separate. Pastors and theologians, the second part of the sentence suggests, are in the best position to untangle the nexus of conflated ideas about the nature of power in order to give women—and, one might add, laymen?—access to a "decision making" institutional power quite separate from a priestly sacramental power. Placed in the context of the passage from the *America* interview on "thinking with the church," the sentence adumbrates a further step in discernment of how all the people of God "walking together" might have a genuine dialogue about what it means to be at once within God's kingdom and assisting in its creation.

The pope ends his apostolic exhortation by holding up Mary as our model in the "new phase of evangelization" that he has urged so eloquently, pointing out the virtues such as humility, tenderness, a contemplative spirit, and an impassioned desire for earthly justice that make her exemplary (*EG* 284-88). In paragraph 286 he makes a brief mention of the events that took place at Cana, describing Mary as "the friend who is ever concerned that wine not be lacking in our lives." But one could add that she shows other qualities as well in the interaction with her Son that leads to his epiphanic first miracle. She is calm, aware, concerned with others' welfare without being self-important or judgmental. She is incisive and decisive: "*Do whatever he tells you,*" she says to the servants (John 2:6). In other words, she shows all the best qualities of a good administrator. So when Mary says quietly to her Son, "They have no wine," she may still be saying to him, "All your people need more ways to express in service their experience of your love."

Contributors

Jerome P. Baggett (Ph.D., Graduate Theological Union and University of California, Berkeley) is Professor of Religion and Society at the Jesuit School of Theology of Santa Clara University. He is the author of *Habitat for Humanity: Building Private Homes, Building Public Religion* and *Sense of the Faithful: How American Catholics Live Their Faith.*

Catherine Cornille (Ph.D., Leuven) is Professor of Comparative Theology at Boston College. She is author of *The Im-Possibility of Interreligious Dialogue* and editor of *Song Divine: Christian Commentaries on the Bhagavad Gita, Criteria of Discernment in Interreligious Dialogue,* and *The World Market and Interreligious Dialogue.*

Paul Crowley, S.J. (Ph.D., Graduate Theological Union) is the Jesuit Community Professor in Religious Studies at Santa Clara University. Specializing in systematic and philosophical theology, he has published several articles and books, including *In Ten Thousand Places: Dogma in a Pluralistic Church.*

David E. DeCosse (Ph.D., Boston College) is Visiting Associate Professor in Religious Studies at Santa Clara University and Director of Ethics Programs for the Markkula Center for Applied Ethics at Santa Clara. He is widely published in the area of social ethics and conscience.

William Ditewig (Ph.D., Catholic University of America) is the Dean's Executive Professor in the Graduate Program of Pastoral Ministries at Santa Clara University. A deacon of the diocese of Monterey, California, he is the author of numerous articles and of several books, the most recent of which (coauthored with Gary Macy and Phyllis Zagano) is *Women Deacons: Past, Present, Future.*

Albert Gelpi (Ph.D., Harvard) is the William Robertson Coe Professor Emeritus of American Literature at Stanford. He also served as Associate Graduate Dean at Stanford. He has published and edited a number of books on American poets and the development of the American poetic tradition.

Barbara Gelpi (Ph.D., Harvard) is Professor Emerita in English at Stanford. She has taught and published in Romantic and Victorian literature and is currently writing about the early years of the Oxford Movement.

Barbara Green, O.P. (Ph.D., Graduate Theological Union and University of California, Berkeley) is Professor of Biblical Studies at the Graduate Theological Union and the Dominican School of Philosophy and Theology. She is the author of *Jonah's Journeys* and, with Catherine Murphy and Carleen Mandolfo, *John's Revelation: The Interfaces Biblical Storyline Companion.*

Kristin Heyer (Ph.D., Boston College) is Bernard J. Hanley Professor in Religious Studies at Santa Clara University. Focusing on social ethics, her books include *Prophetic and Public: The Social Witness of U.S. Catholicism* and *Kinship across Borders: A Christian Ethic of Immigration.*

J. Leon Hooper, S.J. (Ph.D., Boston College) is director of the Woodstock Library at Georgetown University. An expert in the thought of John Courtney Murray, he has published and lectured widely on the topic of Vatican II and religious liberty.

Paul Lakeland (Ph.D., Vanderbilt) is the Aloysius P. Kelley S.J. Professor of Catholic Studies at Fairfield University. He is the author of nine books, including *The Liberation of the Laity: In Search of an Accountable Church, Catholicism at the Crossroads: How the Laity Can*

Save the Church, Church: Living Communion, and, most recently, *A Council That Will Never End: Lumen Gentium and the Church Today.*

Bryan Massingale (S.T.D., Pontifical University Alphonsianum) is Professor of Theological Ethics at Marquette University. He is the author of many articles and of the book *Racial Justice and the Catholic Church.* He is former President of the Catholic Theological Association of America.

John R. Quinn, Archbishop Emeritus of San Francisco, is former President of the United States Conference of Catholic Bishops and the author of several articles and books on the Church. His latest book is *Ever Ancient, Ever New: Structures of Communion in the Catholic Church.*

Stephen R. Schloesser, S.J. (Ph.D., Stanford) is Associate Professor in History at Loyola University of Chicago. Prior to Loyola, he was on the faculty at Boston College. He is the author of *Jazz-Age Catholicism: Mystic Modernism in Postwar Paris, 1919-1933,* and of *Visions of Amen: The Early Life and Work of Olivier Messiaen.*

Sally Vance-Trembath (Ph.D., Notre Dame) is Lecturer in Theology in the Department of Religious Studies at Santa Clara University. She is the author of several articles, including "John Paul II's *Ut unum sint* and the Conversation with Women," *Theological Studies* 60 (1999).

Index